Ed Gl

T0270465

111 Places
in Essex
That You
Shouldn't Miss

Photographs by Karin Tearle

emons:

For Juliet Rose and Simon Rose

© Emons Verlag GmbH
All rights reserved
© Photographs by Karin Tearle, except:
ch. 85, Temple of Concord: © English Heritage
© Cover Icon: private
Layout: Eva Kraskes, based on a design
by Lübbeke | Naumann | Thoben
Maps: altancicek.design, www.altancicek.de
Basic cartographical information from Openstreetmap,
© OpenStreetMap-Mitwirkende, OdbL
Editing: Ros Horton
Printing and binding: Grafisches Centrum Cuno, Calbe
Printed in Germany 2022
ISBN 978-3-7408-1593-6
First edition

Guidebooks for Locals & Experienced Travellers
Join us in uncovering new places around the world at
www.111places.com

Foreword

'Good evening. I'm from Essex, in case you couldn't tell.' Thus begins Ian Dury's unforgettable, unmatchable 'Billericay Dickie' from 1977, just one of a host of his roaring uproarious Rabelaisian song-poems. Can any other British county boast so striking an identity? Such confidence, borne of boastfulness and cockiness. Dury was reminding the rest of Britain what they were missing by failing to cross the Rubicon or, more prosaically, the River Lea from London, to delight in the most misunderstood area in the country.

Yes, Essex is misunderstood because the very mention of its name sends a large part of the British public into paroxysms of laughter and mockery fuelled by Essex Man, Simon Heffer's ingenious invention from 1990 to describe a cocky, coarse, money-grabbing yob, the epitome of Margaret Thatcher's self-made man, and later exacerbated by the frightening, vapid emptiness of the unwatchable TV programme *TOWIE – The Only Way is Essex*. Unfortunate compliments to a county that without such crude delights would still be best known for its famed seaside resorts: coarse Clacton, smashing Southend and frosty Frinton.

To help you find your way around this book, with its emphasis on the quirky and lesser known, locations are listed alphabetically by city, town or village. Places east of the River Lea, the traditional eastern boundary of London, such as East Ham and Ilford, that were wholly Essex until hostile 1960s and 1970s boundary changes messed everything up, are included under the ingenious heading 'London Essex'. That way we can pay tribute to the local setting of one of the world's greatest ever pop songs, the Small Faces' 'Itchycoo Park', and remind ourselves of Essex's great gifts to modern culture: the brash, boorish music of Dr Feelgood and Billy Bragg alongside Ian Dury, those ingenious synth innovators, Basildon's Depeche Mode, and the stately elegiac sea-drenched super-shanties of Southend's Procol Harum.

111 Places

1 Basildon – Birthplace of Essex Man

Welcome to Bas Vegas

It's only five foot, not 45 foot, high and it's not quite as well known as its Beverley Hills' cousin, but nevertheless it's the perfect cinematic, showbizzy welcome to banal Basildon, the 1946 New Town that more than any other (oh, okay, apart from Billericay, Brentwood, Colchester, Southend…did I say Harlow?) sums up everything clichéd about Essex Man: a brash, loud, working-class Tory-voting council house-buying, *Eastenders*-watching white van driving type who has paved over his front garden, placed a barbecue he never uses at the back that he can spot through the French windows, supports West Ham, and has spent more on car speakers than he has on his *motah*.

The concept of Essex Man was invented by the county's greatest modern-day writer, Simon Heffer, in an anonymous column in the *Sunday Telegraph* in October 1990 to describe the demographic phenomenon that had kept Margaret Thatcher in office since 1979 and looked like it would keep her there for ever. Yet, ironically, new Essex towns such as Basildon had grown out of a post-war Labour government ideal of a new classless society framed by council houses, comprehensive schools and skilled manual labour.

The reality would be hideous tower blocks, brutalist concrete shopping precincts, after dark no-go zones, a Wetherspoons rated as the second worst in the county on Tripadvisor, and a leisure park nicknamed 'Bas Vegas'. If that wasn't bad enough, credit experts, Totally Money, recently rated Basildon as the worst town in the whole country for millennials when it came to working hours, earnings, business start-ups and numbers on benefits.

The £90,000 Basildon sign was erected in 2010. Motorists have plenty of time to savour it as the A127 it sits by is one of the most traffic-choked in Essex.

Address Junction of the A 127 and A 176, Basildon, SS 15 4HX | Getting there Train to Basildon | Tip St Martin's Square on the west side of town features the world's first glass bell tower and an unusual statue of Christ.

2 Depeche Who?
'Leave in Silence'

They're massive across Europe and big in Japan. Depeche-mania has acolytes from Saskatchewan to Switzerland via Singapore. There's a bar dedicated to them in Tallin, Estonia. In Moscow every 9 May fans march through the streets in celebration of singer Dave Gahan's birthday. They've sold more than a hundred million records and made some of the most imaginative and ingenious singles in recorded history. Who has never held a loved one or family pet close and not sung: 'All I ever wanted, all I ever needed is here, in my arms'? Who has not rushed onto the dance floor at the first synth sounds of the ecstatic 'Just Can't Get Enough'? Who has never suddenly stopped in the street in awe to ruminate at the lyrical dexterity of 'Everything Counts'?

Yet, in their hometown of Basildon, Depeche Mode are ignored. There are no statues, tributes or street names, no homecoming parades, no guided tours à la 'Joy Division's Manchester'. Clearly, modern music tourism has not caught up with the terminally naff town yet. The music press, easily pleased by violent anti-social rap, rather than acknowledging Depeche Mode's transformation from teenage synth-poppers into dark masters of songs about emotional pain and sexual perversion, have cruelly mocked the electro boys by referring to them as the 'Four Walters from Basildon, representative of the cult of the diamond geezer'.

At least fans keep altering the street sign of The Gore, Basildon, to Martin L. Gore in honour of the band's leading songwriter. To make up for the lack of local official interest, leather-clad goth fans from far-flung foreign parts make the pilgrimage here to find the 'Very Bas' set, who had known the band as contemporaries, to dance to classic electro – Kraftwerk, Erasure, Cabs and of course Mode – at local discos.

As the song goes: 'Words are very unnecessary, they can only do harm'.

Address The Gore, Basildon, SS 14 | **Getting there** Train to Basildon; by car, just north of the A 1321 and Basildon Fire Station | **Tip** The Edge (no relation to the U2 guitarist) is probably the best bar in Basildon for enjoying live music and DJs. Just make sure you ask for 'Songs of Innocence' and 'Songs of Experience'.

3 Weirdness at Wat Tyler

Pleasant, and not too revolting

Wat Tyler Country Park, named after the local-born leader of the Peasants' Revolt, contains an assortment of odd sculptures. *Why?*, yes, just *Why?*, consists of 68 stained wooden figures, 34 male, 34 female, set in an amphitheatre created by walls that are all that remain of an explosives factory. Michael Condron's *Progression* shows three figures helping each other onto a plinth. The steel *Sound Pods* by Natasha Carsberg reveal a spectrum of different noises made by tapping surfaces and blowing through pipes. And to make the obvious connection with the Peasants' Revolt of 1381, there's *After the Uprising*, which recalls how residents from the local marshland villages marched on London to protest against the poll tax. As a tribute, Robert Koenig has carved seven symbolic figures from chestnut trees, one representing Tyler himself.

Other designs include the *White Hart*, a 2002 aluminium, brass and glass sculpture by Robert Worley. The white hart, which gave its name to innumerable pubs, was Richard II's personal animalian symbol – and he was the king who clashed with the peasants. He chose the white hart, a semi-mythical being usually associated with Jesus Christ, because it was a pun on his name: Richard – Rich Heart – White Hart.

Don't forget the Sonic Marshmallows. They were designed by the Troika team in 2006 to create something playful for children and to seize their imagination. Its inspiration is the concrete, coastal, pre-radar sound mirrors that spied on enemy planes. They create a beam of sound allowing a person standing in front to hear somebody's whispers 60 yards away across a pond. The reverse side allows users to spy on people in the car park and animals in the woodland.

But perhaps the strangest object is the huge steel cockroach by Luke Warburton under which the public can shelter to take refuge from the sonic marshmallows and sound pods.

Address Pitsea Hall Lane, Pitsea, Basildon, SS 16 4UH, +44 (0)1268 208090, www.wattylercountrypark.org.uk | Getting there By car, take Pitsea Hall Lane south of the ubiquitous A 13 at a junction near Pitsea railway station | Hours Daily 9am–5pm | Tip Head south towards Holehaven Creek and a bewildering delta of waterways and inlets, the ideal haven for marine explorers.

4 Essex's Noisiest Church

Stop the service, there's a train!

One minute you're kneeling for prayer and in communion with God; the next the service stops because a noisy train has just rolled by, sounding like it was going right through the nave and out of the apse.

Welcome to St Margaret of Antioch, which stands just a few feet from the Fenchurch Street to Shoeburyness line. The church came first, so it really was irresponsible of the railway authorities to build the line there. Although St Margaret's is mostly locked due to vandalism, weddings still take place, and if you're lucky enough to be invited, just think, in the old days of steam, trains going by would blow their whistles if they saw a wedding taking place. Nowadays, if the trains are having a day off, there's always the chance of the spiritual peace being shattered by the noise of tractors.

St Margaret of Antioch is named after the Patron Saint of childbirth and midwifery. It dates back to Saxon times and is recorded in the Domesday Book. An H. W. King from the Essex Archaeological Society moaned back in 1858 that the church had been 'barbarously rebuilt', although he praised Major Spitty who saved the relics and effigies. The tower contains two ancient bells, one inscribed in Longobardic characters. Although the village name sounds like that of James Ward-Prowse's understudy at Southampton – 'Coming on, Number 4, Essex Bowers-Gifford…"Conservative"!' – the name simply means cottages belonging to the lords of the manor, the Giffords.

Nothing much has ever happened here apart from a shocking incident in 1960. Four men in an Austin Mini were travelling after dark from Southend to London when as they approached a junction an articulated lorry pulled up. The driver of the Mini was travelling too fast and didn't see what was blocking his path until it was too late. The car went under the trailer, slicing off its roof, decapitating the men. Although four bodies were found in the car only three heads were ever discovered.

Address Old Church Road, Bowers Gifford, SS 13 2HG, +44 (0)1268 558430 | Getting there By car, take the A 1464 through Bowers Gifford, up a tiny lane, past a farm and round a corner | Hours Viewable from the outside 24 hours and inside during services | Tip Battlesbridge Antiques Centre, a 10-minute drive up the A 10, is packed with charm and curios.

5_ Gant Around Braintree
A mess of pottage

Unique to Braintree, one of Essex's busiest towns, are alleyways named Gants, which twist through buildings towards the old market square, once famous for its sales of cattle. There are eight of them, including Leatherworkers Gant, Bird In Hand Gant, Hilly Gant, and Pig's Head in the Pottage Pot Gant. This last one, dating from 1753, is sort of named after a long-gone inn Dogshead in the Porridge Pott. Hilly Gant connects St Michael's Church to New Street. It is named after St Michael's 16th-century vicar, John Hill, but was originally 'Hell's Gant', as New Street was notorious for its three pubs, The George, The Dragon and The Three Tuns, which were known as 'Little Hell', 'Great Hell', and 'Damnation'.

The word 'Gant' comes from the Flemish for corridor. Flemish weavers brought the term over from the Low Countries when they settled here in the 16th century and made the town a centre for weaving. Braintree had long been a centre for the wool trade, with fulling mills by the Rivers Brain, Pant and Blackwater. In 1452 the Braintree Bailiffs certified that 'the Art of Mystery of weaving woollen cloth' was undertaken locally. When the Flems came, they settled in empty pilgrim hostelries in Bradford Street and produced fine new cloths called bays and says.

A downside in Braintree's story came with religious intolerance that saw many people flee and emigrate to the New World to found Braintree, Massachusetts and Hartford, Connecticut. The rise of the cotton trade in the 18th century spelled the end of the wool trade. Nevertheless, locals responded ingeniously – Braintree turned to silk. In 1799 George Courtauld set up a silk-throwing business, which became one of the most successful industrial stories of the 19th century, especially once a fashion came in for crape (crimped silk gauze), used in mourning and encouraged by Queen Victoria after the death of Albert.

Address Various in Braintree, CM7 | **Getting there** The Gants are about 400 yards north-west of Braintree railway station | **Tip** Paycocke's House is a gorgeous red and white striped half-timbered Tudor merchant's house, five miles east of Braintree, built by wealthy cloth merchant Thomas Paycocke, and now run by the National Trust.

6 Silver End Model Village
When I'm making windows

Essex is one of the most radical counties in England. It's where philanthropists, free thinkers and social innovators have long come to realise their utopian dreams. One such was Francis Henry Crittall, a Braintree ironmonger, who created Silver End model village in Braintree in the 1920s for his workers, particularly to help disabled Great War veterans.

The idea came to him one day when he turned off the road that connected his factories in Braintree and Witham, and spotted this isolated hamlet. 'I reached a small cluster of rural cottages, set among trees and grouped about an inn, and I recognised it from my boyhood as a spot known as Silver End.' Crittall bought the land and opened a factory where he made the striking horizontal metal windows named after him, inspired from the trouble his mother once had dealing with wooden windows. He built Art Deco houses full of light and space that were a marked contrast to cramped insanitary Victorian properties. As architect, he chose the Scot Thomas Tait who later designed the concrete pylons of Sydney Harbour Bridge. The best houses can be found at the end of Silver Street and on Boars Tye Road.

Francis Crittall so cared for his workers he not only paid them handsomely, he devised the first ever five-day week – no more Saturday mornings labouring – realising they would work better if they had two days off. He built what is the largest village hall in the country. It had a quality dance floor, cinema, library, snooker room and health clinic. In 1928, he built a large department store; food was farmed locally; there was even a sausage factory, so locals had no need to go anywhere else for anything. Silver End was so successful half the population of Braintree was made up of his workers and their families.

In 2006, production ceased at the original Crittall site, although the window frames are still manufactured in Witham.

Address Silver End, Witham, Braintree, CM8 3RQ | Getting there Train to Witham or White Notley; by car, take the A 120 to Braintree McDonald's, then head south-east along Long Green for nearly two miles | Tip Hedingham Castle, 10 miles north of Braintree, features the best-preserved Norman keep in England, and was where Matilda, occasional 12th century Queen of England, died of the fever.

7 _ Kelvedon Hatch Bunker
Your air is beautiful tonight – atomic

World War II is over (it's 1945) and the next war will obviously be an atomic war. So it is vital that the authorities build a huge atomic bunker way below ground to save the government and the most important people from destruction.

That is why Kelvedon Hatch, 23 miles north-east of Whitehall, was dug. It had to be in the countryside because London would be destroyed. Not so badly that it couldn't be rebuilt, as were Nagasaki and Hiroshima, but uninhabitable for about a year. That was their thinking in the 1950s. Where better to create the nuclear bunker than hidden away in a wood off the A 128 near Ongar station, the London Underground system's most obscure outpost, its very existence a running joke in the capital, and so a compulsory purchase order was slapped on farmland.

The public were told Kelvedon Hatch was an air defence station, R4 Sector Operations Control, as part of the RAF's ROTOR air defence project. In secret, they dug 125 feet underground with an entrance through what looks like a bungalow leading to a 100-yard-long tunnel. The bunker had air-conditioning (not much use), heating, cooling, its own water supply, generators and even its own operating theatre. However, it was decommissioned – spoilsports – in 1992. According to official sources this was because the nuclear threat had by then diminished. But who believes official sources? In reality the bunker was decommissioned because the nuclear bombs were now so powerful, so cataclysmic, that if one dropped on London everything here would be incinerated immediately and any bunker would be as much use as a chocolate fireguard.

After being decommissioned, the land was sold back to the original owners, the Parrish family. It is now a tourist attraction and often used for filming. Kelvedon Hatch is easy to find: the area is filled with tourist signs directing people to the 'secret' nuclear bunker.

Address Crown Buildings, Kelvedon Hall Lane, Kelvedon Hatch, CM14 5TL, +44 (0)1277 364883, www.secretnuclearbunker.com | Getting there By car, take the A 128, Ongar Road, five miles north from Brentwood | Hours 1 Mar–31 Oct 10am–4pm weekdays, 10am–5pm weekends & bank holidays; 1 Nov–end Feb Thu–Sun 10am–4pm | Tip Head towards the M11 for the North Weald Airfield to hear about its role in the war and civil defence.

8 *TOWIE*'s Sugar Hut

Surely there must be another way for Essex?

If Essex didn't have enough image problems, in 2010 along came one of the most gut-wrenching, nail-scraping TV programmes in media history: the barely believable, unwatchable reality show *The Only Way Is Essex*.

The premise was simple. Gather together a group of vacuous beautiful people and have them talk unreconstructed codswallop in a series of vacuous beautiful homes or here in the Sugar Hut nightclub. It was billed as 'real people in modified situations, saying unscripted lines but in a structured way'.

The contrived scenes usually involved a middle-aged brute of a man in ridiculously tight Stone Island jeans spilling his heart out to his son – even tighter jeans, plucked eyebrows, ultra-shiny shoes, reeking of Terre d'Hermes – with a conversation that went something like: 'I've nefer before told anyone about mah feelin's, but son, I luff yew.' Cue: tears, big hugs and slaps followed by half an hour chat about West Haaam. Later, the action moves to the Sugar Hut club, 'baroque and Asian decor in a 15th-century coaching inn', where Essex Man meets Essex Girl, a barely believable phenomenon made of peroxide blonde strands, white stiletto heels, fake tan, and a chalkboard-scraping estuary accent.

Why Brentwood? Well, Frank Lampard, the ultimate Essex upstart, went to school here and scooped 10 O-Levels. The main *TOWIE* stars have been Mark Wright, who made 10 appearances for top football club Crawley Town, and even married the Northern equivalent of the Essex girl, *Coronation Street*'s Michelle Keegan, and James Argent, so absurdly well dressed, he put Ernest Marples to shame. Such is the popularity of *TOWIE*, stag and hen parties make the pilgrimage every weekend, enticed by the prospect of meeting a cast member and even going on car tours. Suffice to say it's not quite *The South Bank Show* with Melvyn Bragg on the propositions of Wittgenstein.

Address The Sugar Hut, 93 High Street, Brentwood, CM14 4RR, +44 (0)1277 402293, www.thesugarhut.co.uk | Getting there The club is a mile north of Brentwood railway station | Hours Normal club hours – check website | Tip Where else, but the Blue Boar, Mark Wright's local, in Abridge, the village itself the traditional home for West Ham stars, from Ronnie Boyce to David Moyes?

9__ Tiles of the Shipwrecked

Tributes to the sank of cinque

The sailing mecca of Brightlingsea has the distinction of being the only town associated with the Cinque Ports outside Kent and Sussex. These ports were obliged to provide ships and men to fight for the king, but their role is now purely ceremonial. Schoolchildren are reminded that the name comes from the French for five, not because all the boats that left their shores sank.

One of Brightlingsea's most striking features is the set of 213 tiles in the church of All Saints. They are dedicated to parishioners who lost their lives at sea in 1872 when the storms were so severe they caused widespread destruction. That year, 36 local seamen met their end in Davy Jones' locker. To commemorate them the vicar, the Rev Arthur Pertwee, created a frieze of individual tiles, each inscribed with the deceased's name and their ship. Indeed, the good reverend was such a fisherman's friend, he would climb to the top of the tower and place a light on the flagstaff to guide the fleet safely home in a storm.

The number of tiles has since increased from 36, because when a Brightlingsea native is lost at sea, a tile is usually added. These include one for Sidney Siebert, not a fisherman, but a victim of the *Titanic*, but not one for the sailors from the wrecked yacht *Lorena* in 1903 who are buried in an unmarked mass grave in the churchyard.

Brightlingsea was an island, surrounded by creeks and inlets, until the 16th century. It is big in the oyster world and for many years was twinned with French oyster fishery port Marennes, Charente-Maritime. A downside was that the port was used for exporting live animals to be slaughtered, resulting in many protest campaigns. The ancient ceremonies still take place: every year on the first Monday after St Andrew's Day, 'Choosing Day', the Freemen of Brightlingsea gather to elect a Deputy to represent the Mayor of Sandwich.

Address All Saints Church, Movers Lane, Brightlingsea, Colchester, CO7 0RZ, +44 (0)1206 302407, www.allsaintswithjamesb-sea.co.uk | Getting there The church is about a mile north of the village off the B 1029 | Hours Contact the church for up-to-date information | Tip Brightlingsea was one of the first outposts of the nonconformist Protestant cult of Swedenborgianism in the early 19th century. The first local chapel was built in 1814 in New Street and is now a private house. The second, from the 1860s, is in Queen Street.

The sea

ROBERT TAYLOR
aged · 57
Master · of · the
Ketch · Antelope
drowned · in · Brith · Dock
Ian · 24 · 1886

ROBERT DEATH
aged · 37
Drowned · off · Southport
from · the · Yacht · Autoun
June · 3rd · 1886
and · buried · at · Southport

WILLIAM HENRY WEBB
aged · 22
lost · in · the · Emigrant · Ship
Kapunda
off · the · Coast · of · Brazil
Ian · 20 · 1887

10_ The Hostage Windows

Stained glass celebrates freedom from captivity

Two stained-glass windows in the church of St Mary the Virgin, situated in the small hamlet of Broxted in wonderful countryside, commemorate one of the most infamous international political events of the 1980s: the capture and eventual freedom of the local journalist John McCarthy after being kidnapped by Islamic terrorists in April 1986.

McCarthy was a 29-year-old television journalist snatched at gunpoint by Jihadists in Beirut on his first foreign assignment. In Lebanon he became Britain's longest-held hostage, chained by his ankles in a small cramped cell with fellow hostage Brian Keenan with no one in Britain knowing if they were even alive. Then, one day in August 1991, without warning, his captors confiscated his radio and began to unlock his shackles. After five years or 1,943 days in captivity, during which time his girlfriend, Jill Morrell, had launched the group 'Friends of John McCarthy', he was freed. A Test match was halted to announce the news and tube passengers burst into tears.

When McCarthy returned home he discovered his mother Sheila had died of cancer. A service was held in St Mary's to mark his release and a pair of Victorian windows was replaced with John Clark's moving stained glass, dedicated not just to McCarthy's plight but to all hostages. Information panels explain the symbolism of the scenes and how the artist worked with John McCarthy to create them.

The 13th-century church stands in an ancient enclosure that might have been a Celtic holy site. Pieces of Roman brick have been inserted into the east wall of the chancel. The Captivity Window is mostly black and white, with only a few splashes of colour. But the Freedom Window is ablaze, representing the release of the hostages and McCarthy's desire for reconciliation and peace. Robert Runcie, Archbishop of Canterbury, was meant to perform the dedication but broke his ankle.

Address Church End Villas, Broxted, Dunmow, CM6 2BU, +44 (0)1371 856080,
www.thefiveparishes.org.uk | Getting there Broxted is three miles north-east of Stansted
Airport, just off the B 1051 | Hours Open daily during daylight hours, but this can vary
so best to phone | Tip Given Broxted's location, the obvious diversion must be to do some
serious plane spotting around Stansted. Belmer Road is your best bet.

11 Le Corbusier-Styled Yacht Club

Towards a new architecture

The wind wisping through your hair, the smack of the waves against the hull, the smell of the salty sea spray, a blue and white striped top and peaked cap, the spirit of Ted Heath. Yachting on a smooth serene North Sea – what could be more exhilarating? It's one of the most popular pastimes past Pitsea and Prittlewell and has drawn in the unlikeliest of adherents, even the great novelist Arnold Bennett, who kept his beloved Dutch yacht in waters here.

To indulge at the top end of the sailing game it has to be Burnham-on-Crouch. In 1931, the glitterati and yachterati created *the* most magnificent glittering maritime palace, the Royal Corinthian Yacht Club. Steel, glass, clean, white, fresh, translucent by Joseph Emberton, a progressive designer working during the golden period of English architecture, who had not only swotted up on *Vers Une Architecture* by Le Corbusier, the master, but had even translated it into English in 1927. Emberton also designed the celebrated Simpson's store on London's Piccadilly, now the universe's biggest Waterstone's.

There was, however, a downside. The leading American architect Philip Johnson, a co-curator of the exhibition, blasted the 'extraordinarily bad circular staircase which you were probably forced to use'. He might have added that white modernism by the sea looks glorious under a blue sky but gradually starts to fade after long winters buffeted by the easterly winds.

The reputation of Burnham-on-Crouch as a sophisticated stylish setting took a bash in 1977 with Ian Dury's hilarious song, 'Billericay Dickie', in which a possible paramour approaches the anti-hero with 'Oh golly, oh gosh, Come and lie on the couch, With a nice bit of posh, From Burnham-on-Crouch'.

Address The Quay, Burnham-on-Crouch, CM0 8AX, +44 (0)1621 782105, www.royalcorinthian.co.uk | Getting there The club is by the Crouch Estuary; train to Burnham-on-Crouch, then a short walk | Hours The club is private but the external architecture can be appreciated at any time | Tip The Clockwork Hotel at 12 Station Road is a bit unusual. Patrons have an hour to find their keys as part of an immersive game. You have to be there really.

12   Art Deco Island Icon
Mighty modernist masterpiece

Even those who have never been to Canvey know exactly what it's all about: the very essence of working-class London overspill coarseness dominated by Harry Enfield Essex Man types, set on a mud-flat prone to flooding, cut off from civilisation. Which explains the shock of finding a growing and accepted Chassidic Jewish community, a fiercely proud music heritage (around the Thames Delta), and the most bio-diverse habitat in the country that includes an RSPB bird sanctuary.

Canvey has also attracted high end designers, architects and engineers, enticed by the light, the water, the ozone. And when it comes to engineers, none was more fêted in the 20th century than Ove Arup, purveyor of 'total architecture', co-creator of Sydney Opera House, but more importantly the brains behind Canvey's Labworth Café, the only building he designed solely, which went up from 1932 – 33, and which was meant to resemble the bridge of the RMS *Queen Mary*.

The gleaming modernist marvel, part of a project to replace the long seawall at Canvey Island, sits on the waterfront wall. Owing to the marshy nature of the soil, the whole structure had to be set on solid concrete piles. Arup worked for the firm of Christiani & Nielsen, who specialised in harbour and quayside projects, and the commission thereby satisfied Arup's long-held plans about collaboration between architect and engineer.

Nevertheless, Arup later expressed misgivings about the project and criticised the company's workmanship, and the cheapness and shoddiness of the materials. Major alterations to the building took place after the floods of 1953 that claimed 58 lives. The building started to suffer neglect as the traditional English seaside holiday began to suffer in the 1970s. It narrowly escaped demolition during redevelopment of the island's sea defences at that time, but Labworth is still in use as a restaurant today.

Address Furtherwick Road, Canvey Island, SS 8 7DW, +44 (0)1268 683209, www.thelabworthcafe.co.uk | Getting there The building is on the sea front at the south of the island to the east of Thorney Bay | Hours Café Tue–Sun 9am–3pm; restaurant Tue–Sat 6pm–midnight | Tip Check out the nearby Canvey seawall, which is adorned with wonderfully creative murals and paintings.

13__ The Chassidim of Canvey
Be fruitful and multiply

It's one of the unlikeliest migrations in recent English history. In 2016, hundreds of ultra-orthodox or Chassidic Jews began to leave Stamford Hill in north London and head 40 miles east along the Thames to unloved Canvey and found a new settlement. House prices had exploded in London and the Chassidim have large families. Various locations, such as Harlow and Milton Keynes, were considered, but who could resist the siren call of the sea even though the last organised Jewish community had withered away in the 1930s.

The exodus from Stamford Hill was carried out in Biblical fashion, but instead of traipsing around the Sinai Peninsula for 40 years, the new wanderers spent 40 minutes in their Volvos negotiating the North Circular, followed by a swift sojourn along the A 13 and across the Hadleigh Ray. Not quite the River Jordan.

The devout Jews' arrival shocked the insular locals, but their very confidence and affability soon assuaged concerns, as did the realisation that the new arrivals' aspirational outlook was similar to that of the islanders whose families had left the choking claustrophobia of London's East End a few generations earlier. Jacob Gross, now the director of Canvey Island's Jewish community, explained to the media how his family moved out of a 'cramped two-bedroom home into a mansion: six bedrooms, big kitchen, massive garden. We feel much more welcome here than a religious Jew in Israel, who feels threatened there. We're opening new horizons and we hope that this will be one example among other places that will start to grow'.

The first six houses on the island were bought in 2016. The following year a Chassidic philanthropist put up £1.75 million to buy an abandoned school, kosher stores were established, and a Swiss-sponsored yeshiva (rabbi training school) opened its doors there. By 2020 there were more than 100 homes and 75 families.

Address There is a kosher store on Meppel Avenue, Canvey Island, SS8 9RZ, +44 (0)7833 433507, and other nearby shops of a similar nature | **Getting there** Meppel Avenue is just north of the B1014, halfway between Castle Point Golf Course and Canvey Island Rugby Club | **Hours** Canvey Kosher is open Sun–Tue 8.30am–8pm, Wed & Thu 8.30am–11pm, Fri 8.30am–3pm | **Tip** There are more churches than synagogues in Canvey, although that might change soon. St Nicholas on the S130 in the middle of the island is the parish church.

14 Dr Feelgood's Surgery
They did it right

The Mississippi has its delta, which gave birth to the blues, and the Thames has this delta, the host of inlets and sand creeks on the way to Southend, which gave birth to rough, raw, back-to-basics roots rock in the 1970s. And no group better summed up the adrenalin-rush spirit of the times than Canvey's Dr Feelgood, who met here at the Monico.

Dr Feelgood couldn't lose. Powered by the formidable rhythm section of bassist John B. Sparks, who followed Willie Dixon's mantra, 'keep it simple, keep it solid', drummer The Big Figure (to the surprise of his mum), formidable guitarist Wilko Johnson, he of the manic stare and blitzkrieg attack, and the even more formidable vocalist Lee Brilleaux, a man who had clearly swallowed razor blades and Jack Daniel's bottles in sounding like an estuary Tom Waits.

They looked as if they were coming off a bank job, but the songs… ah the songs. 'She Does It Right' and 'Roxette' were driven by a manic surge of energy, powerful enough to light up the oil wells of nearby Coryton. Indeed, Julien Temple's 2009 biographical film of the band was called *Oil City Confidential* and reviews noted how their music captured the barminess of Canvey where caravan parks sit by petrochemical plants and children paddle in the river as huge cargo ships glide by.

The Monico is one of a number of early 20th-century whiter-than-white Art Deco Canvey buildings. Special planning permission had to be sought in creating it, for the beach is only 75 yards away and the cellar 16 feet below the high water level. Seven thousand cubic yards of soil were extracted, but amazingly not one stone was found. The Monico boasts a unique privilege: by agreement with the port authorities its illuminated sign is kept on after closing time to aid ships. Unfortunately, the building's reputation has declined since the days when it was Dr Feelgood's surgery.

Address The Monico, 4 Eastern Esplanade, Canvey Island, SS8 7DL, +44 (0)1268 683026, www.visitingcanvey.co.uk | **Getting there** The Monico is on the south side of the island, by the junction of Furtherwick Road and the Eastern Esplanade, just east of Central Park | **Hours** Sun–Thu noon–11pm, Fri & Sat noon–2am (but hours can vary depending on the weather, so best to telephone first) | **Tip** Looking for more fun? It's a short walk to Fantasy Island amusement park.

15 Dutch Cottages of 1618
Nether nether land

They look like contenders for Tom Thumb's country retreat, but they are simply 400-year-old dwelling places built in the vernacular style then popular in Holland. Helpful ditch and dyke builders from across the North Sea settled in Canvey throughout the 17th century and built a number of similar properties, but only these two survive. One is a private residence; the other is a museum run by Castle Point Borough Council.

They were led by Cornelius Vermuyden who had been commissioned by the Crown to drain Hatfield Chase in the Isle of Axholme, Lincolnshire, after which he and his colleagues came to Canvey, although not without a bit of argy-bargy from the locals. Vermuyden and Co. drained and embanked the land, and introduced such skilled land reclamation methods to England, constructing washes to allow periodic flooding of the area by excess waters, that he was knighted in 1629, becoming an English citizen in 1633.

But even Vermuyden could not counteract seasonal Canvey flooding, given that the island is only two feet above sea level, and such flooding could not be controlled properly until the creation of steam-powered pumps in the 19th century, and the construction of additional water control projects in the 1960s. The worst Canvey flood was in January 1953 when a tidal surge broke through the sea wall on the northern side of the island, killing 60 people in a community of only 8,000. Many died of hypothermia while sitting on the roof of their bungalows. Communications were so terrible it took an age for back-up services to realise how bad things were.

The properties were given to Canvey Island Urban District Council in 1952, and subsequently restored, repainted and reroofed with thatch ready for opening as a museum in 1962. Inside are exhibits about the history of Canvey Island itself, including models of sailing craft from Roman times.

Address Dutch Cottage Museum, 1618 Canvey Road, Canvey Island, SS 8 0QP, +44 (0)1268 882200 | **Getting there** Canvey Road leads straight south from Benfleet station just over a mile away | **Hours** Spring Bank Holiday to Sept, Wed, Sat & Sun 2.30 – 5pm; Bank Holidays 10am – 1pm & 2 – 5pm | **Tip** Continue south along Canvey Road to the twee and welcoming Heritage Centre built into the old St Katherine's Church, which dates back to 1628 when Dutch labourers petitioned the king that they might hold services in their own language.

16 Last Degaussing Station
Still in the loop

It's right next to the council toilets, which is perhaps not the best recommendation, on the east side of Thorney Bay, and it looks a bit odd. It used to have a sign saying *Ministry of Defence Property*. In the late 1980s it was still listed in the Private MOD internal phone directory and remained a UK Admiralty Secret site until 1993. It's even got a balcony for clear views across the estuary, or at least until a new, higher sea wall was built.

Okay, it's now simply the Bay Museum, but the more interesting story is that it is an old Cold War magnetic degaussing loop station. Indeed, it is the last remaining complete World War II degaussing station on the north side of the Thames. Its creation all stemmed from the danger of magnetic sea mines, a huge problem for ships, which had to be degaussed or, in plain English, de-magnetised, to prevent the mines detecting them. Cables ran from the building under the Thames.

The station was built from 1962–63 at the height of the Cold War following the Cuban Missile Crisis, which some believe nearly ended with a nuclear missile exchange between NATO and the Eastern Bloc. Nuclear defences were then reinforced and to add the icing onto the atomic cake other facilities were added, such as this – the Canvey Loop, so named because two thick loops of cable sat on the river bed below the shipping. Any vessel that passed would induce small currents into the loops of cable that could then be detected back here. Indeed, the wire still remains on the seabed.

Fortunately, the nuclear threat diminished – or so we're led to believe – and the conspicuously secret site was shut. Reopened as a museum, it now houses military memorabilia, and contains features on local and world military history. The volunteers also organise trips to France and Belgium to visit old battlefields and help people research their own family military histories.

Address The Bay Museum, The Old Degaussing Station, 3 Cleveland Road, Canvey Island SS8 0AY, www.the-bay-museum.co.uk | Getting there The museum is at the north-east side of Thorney Bay in the centre of the southern side of the island | Hours Sun & Bank Holidays 10am–4pm | Tip Head to nearby Southend to take a boat trip for an unrivalled view of Canvey on the north side of the estuary and Kent on the south side.

17___Lobster Smack
Smuggle yourself inside

Right by the foaming estuary at the very edge of Canvey is this seafood-serving ex-smugglers' stamping ground. Originally it was the World's End. Indeed, a version of the pub has been here since the 1580s. The clientele were sailors, those looking to indulge in bare-knuckle fighting in the yard, and smugglers. Okay, no smuggling takes place any more – so the authorities hope – but it did when Charles Dickens used it as the model for the Sluice House in *Great Expectations* (1861), where Pip is jumped after walking through the rain-soaked marshes in the dark.

Historically, Canvey was a marshy backwater populated mostly by sheep but much visited by those who preferred their baccy not be taxed by The Man. Secret chambers and subterranean passages led from the shore to the local parish church, allowing the tax avoiders to say a quick prayer before escaping with their dodgy goods, mostly tea, rum, brandy and woollen cloth. There was no fresh water on Canvey; ewe's milk, used to make cheese, was used for bartering. To make it as difficult as possible for the smugglers, the Hovering Act of 1718 made it illegal for ships lighter than 50 tons to moor within six miles of the shore.

Low-lying Canvey Island was perfectly placed for such activity. Ships could be easily unloaded and swag brought onto the island before the smugglers headed west to London where taxes were levied. On the way back, they could stop again to load up with wool, the export of which was forbidden in 1660. Nevertheless, fleeces from England were smuggled to Flanders in their thousands.

Imports, exports, pfaff! Taxes went up – what a surprise! – first to fund the 100 Years Wars with France from 1337 and then again in war after war. As recently as 25 years ago, 570 kilos of tobacco were seized from a yacht in nearby Holehaven Creek. And the penalty for smuggling (but not now)? Death by hanging.

Address Haven Road, Canvey Island, SS8 0NR, +44 (0)1268 514297, www.classicinns.co.uk/thelobstersmackcanveyisland | Getting there The pub is at the south-western tip of the island | Hours Sun–Thu 11am–11pm, Fri & Sat 11am–midnight | Tip Fancy a Canvey pub crawl? It's a long way east along the waterfront to the bars of the Western and Eastern esplanades.

18 Graham Gooch to Bat
Still not out

Graham Gooch, one of England's greatest ever batsmen, is captured for ever in John Doubleday's statue in Chelmsford, where his county, Essex, play. Gooch, born on the London-Essex border at Whipps Cross, Walthamstow, made his Test debut in the 1975 Ashes at Edgbaston, Birmingham, when only 21. He went on to captain not only Essex but England as well in a glorious career that saw him become the most prolific run scorer of all time with a tally of 67,057 first-class runs. He is one of only 25 players to have scored over 100 first-class centuries.

Yet his Test career began against Australia, no less, ingloriously – he was out for a pair – which in non-cricket English means two scores of nought, about as bad as it gets, the only thing worse being out for nought first ball twice. England were humiliated, losing by an innings and 85 runs. Gooch was not put off. His scoring rate for Essex meant that he could not be ignored and he returned to the international fold successfully, being awarded Wisden's Cricketer of the Year in 1980.

Two years later in 1982 things went very wrong. Gooch joined the rebels on a banned tour of apartheid South Africa. All the players concerned were banned from official Test cricket for three years. Gooch, as captain, received the most vilification. Nevertheless, he went on to become the third highest Test run scorer for England. He played for his country for an astonishing 22 years, retiring at the ripe old age of 42.

Gooch was the dupe in one of the most bizarre sporting capers ever witnessed. During the 1991 Ashes Down Under, when he was the relentless sergeant-major England captain, two team-mates, David Gower and John Morris, left the Queensland ground, hopped on a Tiger Moth plane at the nearby airfield, and flew low over the field of action for a laugh. Gower and Morris were banned. King Gooch was not amused.

Address County Place, Chelmsford, CM2 0RE | **Getting there** The statue is just off the A 1060 by the Count Court | **Hours** Accessible 24 hours | **Tip** The Queen's Head pub on Lower Anchor Street, a no-frills, proper local, is the watering-hole for the Essex county cricket ground, which is just 300 yards away.

19 Oldest Wireless Factory
Radio, Live Transmission

Charles Dickens slammed Chelmsford, the county town of Essex, as the dullest and most stupid place on Earth after failing to find a newspaper on a Sunday morning. Perhaps he should have waited for the radio to be invented, for Chelmsford is home to the world's oldest wireless factory.

It all dates back to the arrival of the medium's inventor, Guglielmo Marconi, an Italian of Irish descent, in England in 1896 when he was 21. Marconi had the time and money to indulge in experiments owing to family largesse from the Jameson whiskey company. News came to William Preece, chief engineer to the General Post Office, who asked for a demonstration of the Italian's remarkable new invention. Marconi soon received so many contracts he needed a permanent factory, and took over this old silk mill in December 1898.

Why Chelmsford? It was near but not in London and therefore out of the spotlight. It was also outside the General Post Office's monopoly over Telegraphic Communications. It was near electrical power plants, there was a ready supply of skilled workers, there were no electric trams to interfere with radio signals, and Essex being flat aided the primitive technology.

Here, they made maritime SOS equipment that was later vital in rescuing passengers from stricken ships. However, the Hall Street factory was soon considered too small and a new plant went up in nearby New Street. As this second site went up, the *Titanic* sank, which added considerable weight to the argument that all large ships should be equipped with a Marconi Wireless system.

Dame Nellie Melba took part in the first public display of the new technology in June 1920 when she sang two arias to the world. The signal was received not just throughout Europe but as far away as Newfoundland. The Marconi company went through several corporate hands and is now part of the Swedish firm Ericsson.

MARCONI'S WIRELESS TELEGRAPH CO LTD WORKS

HALL STREET

Address Hall Street, Chelmsford, CM2 0HG | Getting there The old factory is just south of the A 1060, near Chelmsford Presbyterian Church; train to Chelmsford | Hours The factory has been developed and divided into flats – viewable from the outside only | Tip Head to Marconi's second factory on New Street, built on the site of Essex's first county cricket ground.

20   Dickens' Maypole Pub

Sheesh, it's now a kebab joint!

To Charles Dickens, it was 'such a delicious old inn opposite the churchyard', and he featured it as the Maypole in his 1841 novel *Barnaby Rudge*, waxing over 'its overhanging storeys, drowsy little panes of glass, and front bulging out'. According to one authority, the pub represented olde England – 'self-satisfied, comfortable, traditional, moribund'. In reality the Maypole was the mock Tudor black-and-white fronted Olde King's Head, built in 1547, although which old king it referred to was never explained, and it was a secret meeting place for Roundheads during the English Civil War. It is now the Sheesh kebab joint.

Writing to his biographer, John Forster, Dickens remarked that 'Chigwell is the greatest place in the world. The pub has more gable ends than a lazy man would care to count on a sunny day.' Mind you, he described everywhere in similar terms – apart from Chelmsford. *Barnaby Rudge* is one of Dickens' most brutal novels, for it deals with the most violent event in London history: the Gordon Riots of June 1780 when the public raged against giving rights to Catholics. In a later, real-life, political setting the pub was a favourite of mid-20th-century local MP, the quite well-known Winston Churchill.

Barnaby Rudge begins and ends at the Maypole. Chigwell's mention in the novel is the locale's only inclusion in anything that could be vaguely described as cultural. Yet this is one of the richest communities in the country: the area between Chigwell, Buckhurst Hill and Loughton is called the Golden Triangle on account of the property prices. There is only limited public transport because nearly everybody has a Rolls-Royce. An evening out might be topped off by the thrill of bumping into a gangland boss, some *TOWIE* stars, or Harry Kane.

The building was recently bought by local overlord Lord Sugar. Everything inside is black-and-white with a splash of bling.

Address Sheesh, 70 High Road, Chigwell, IG7 6QA, +44 (0)205 5591155, www.sheeshrestaurant.co.uk | Getting there The restaurant is about 300 yards north of Chigwell station and 500 yards east of the M11, just north of the B170 | Hours Restaurant Sun–Thu noon–11.30pm, Fri & Sat noon–10.30pm; bar Sun–Wed noon–11.30pm, Thu–Sat noon–midnight | Tip Leave soulless suburbia behind and head for the wilds of Epping Forest – well, as wild as it gets for outer London.

21 House on Legs
On our block, all of the guys call her flamingo

It looks like it is about to take off, hover over the beach, and end up on its back kicking its legs in the air. But Redshanks is just a house. Okay, just about big enough to satisfy a large, lazy cat, but unlike most British houses it is reached by ladders on one of the remotest beaches in the country. Prosaically, it is an artist's studio in a cork-clad cabin above a tidal salt marsh in Lee-over-Sands.

It was designed by Lisa Shell Architects for sculptor Marcus Taylor who wanted a peaceful place that he could retreat to and where he could concentrate on his work. Inspiration came from oil rigs, wading birds, and in particular Maunsell Forts, the armed towers in the Thames and Mersey estuaries created during World War II to defend the coast. But it's also supposed to depict a 1920s-styled rundown, timber-framed house brought into the hi-tech age.

The locale is on the exposed side of the sea wall. Ordinary houses can be troubled by water at high tide, hence stilts are a clever alternative. Shell herself has explained how 'the coastal site is an extreme environment in which to build, but one that is delicate and sensitive'.

There followed this unique design for Redshanks: three galvanised steel legs coated with a resinous paint to withstand the salty air, lapped by the wash and rush of the sea underneath. The colour of the building's painted pillars refers to the red legs of the redshank – a much-spotted local wading bird. The house on legs demonstrates how to survive the risk of floods with storms and tidal surges rife, while showing respect for the natural environment and not offending the locals. Redshanks even made it to the longlist for the 2017 RIBA House of the Year award. Lee-over-Sands, where Redshanks lives, is a remote hamlet of 34 properties on Colne Point, in between Mersea Island and Clacton-on-Sea, based in a 750-acre bird reserve.

Address Beach Road, Lee-over-Sands, Clacton, CO16 8EX | Getting there There isn't much choice: head south from St Osyth (which is 5 miles west of Clacton) along Beach Road, just about the only route available | Hours Viewable from the outside only | Tip Head north back to the village of St Osyth, pronounced 'Toosey', officially the driest recorded place in the United Kingdom, with an average annual rainfall of just 20 inches.

22 Jaywick Shanty Town
Forlorn and forgotten

It's England's most deprived community. In nearly all official surveys for deprivation, Jaywick is in the relegation zone, often finishing bottom. Nearly three-quarters of residents receive benefits, compared with 15 per cent nationwide. Indeed, 40 per cent of residents are unable to work, due to disability or long-term illness, while 60 per cent of pupils at the local primary school receive free school meals. People come from afar, drawn by its reputation, horrified by the bags of rubbish lying around, and because it's 'so rough'.

How did Jaywick end up in this state? Blame the leading Victorian intellectual William Morris. As a reaction to out-of-control development in the growing cities, he proposed the utopian idea of self-sufficient communities for poor families away from cities. Property developer Frank Stedman built Jaywick in 1928 as a cheap holiday retreat for Londoners in the wake of the success of nearby Clacton as a holiday resort. He offered small plots of land for as little as £25 on what was salt marsh, unsuitable for agriculture, to East Enders desperate to get away from the teeming slums of Shadwell and head to the sea.

The dream was sold with the promise of health, fitness and outdoor exercise. Bizarrely, the original estate was developed in the shape of a car radiator grille with roads named after vehicle manufacturers. After all, this was the new age of the open road, shiny metal, and grown men in shorts.

Initially, Jaywick was a popular holiday destination, but then came war, after which a shortage of housing back in London E1 saw the properties become permanent homes, despite not being built for that purpose – after all, mains sewers were not installed until 1977. The area has since deteriorated further, but locals have resisted demolition and even won a preservation order in 1970. Flooding is an ever-present risk. Strewth.

Address CO15, two miles west of Clacton-on Sea | Getting there The easiest way is to head west from Clacton itself on Marine Parade West and West Road | Hours Accessible 24 hours | Tip Head for Clacton itself, which features one of the best beaches on Essex's Sunshine Coast.

23__Martello Tower Art Centre

Art attack is the best form of defence

Ingenious use has been made of Jaywick Martello Tower. Clacton has turned it into an arts and heritage space where the exhibitions focus on the local, coastal environment and history. There is a year-round programme of talks, workshops and events, and the building acts as a central hub for the local community. The Tower has been a finalist for the Essex Tourism and Hospitality Awards in the Best Small Attraction category.

Military buffs will marvel at the origins of the building. It was built as a Napoleonic Fort in the early 19th century, one of a series, to protect the coast from French invasion. After all, the Essex coast has always been vulnerable to attack from ne'er-do-wells wading through the German Ocean. They were called Martello Towers as inspiration came from the ruins of the Torre della Mortella, a circular fortress in Corsica that held off British attack for several days until it was eventually captured. The attackers were so impressed by its defensive capabilities that they adopted and adapted the design.

As a result, 29 similar defensive fortresses were built starting in 1808, from Point Clear near St Osyth here to Aldeburgh in Suffolk, some of which can still be seen. These towers were round, more than 10 yards high, with walls two to three yards thick. One million bricks, made in Essex at Grays, were used in the construction of each, aided by sand and shingle taken from the nearby beach. They were armed with up to three large guns and smaller cannon. In the end, they were never needed and technology moved on.

A current tenant with a suitable military background is the East Essex Aviation Society, which has a museum here. They were inspired by the recovery of a crashed American P51 Mustang forced to ditch into the sea off the coast of Clacton in January 1945. The Tower has been the ideal place to store and preserve the recovered wreckage.

Address The Promenade, Belsize Avenue, Clacton-on-Sea, CO15 2LF, +44 (0)1255 822783, www.explore-essex.com | Getting there There aren't many roads around here, so take the A 133 towards the sea, head west along St John's Road and south along Jaywick Lane | Hours Apr–Sept Thu–Sun 10am–4pm, Oct–Mar weekends only 10am–4pm | Tip Head west along the sands to St Osyth Beach Sunday Market.

24 Balkerne Gate

Entrance to England's longest Roman town wall

It's no surprise that Colchester boasts of some of the best Roman remains in Britain. The city prides itself as being the oldest in the country, and was indeed a former capital before London. This, the first century Balkerne Gate, was built in A.D. 70–96 as the main entrance into what was the Roman town of Camulodunum. It has four gates and unusually wide carriageways, and is also part of the longest unbroken stretch of Roman town wall in northern Europe, stretching for more than a mile and a half.

Colchester became Roman with Emperor Claudius' invasion in A.D. 43. He built a fortress that was occupied for six years, the lime for making mortar coming from Kent. Colchester became the first of four colonies or *coloniae*, the others being Lincoln, Gloucester and York. So that no one would forget the great emperor, his associates built a huge temple to him after his death, whose foundations can still be seen beneath the Norman castle to the east.

What could go wrong? In A.D. 60 or 61, Boadicea, Queen of the Iceni, launched a revolt while the legions were away. Nevertheless, Colchester was re-established as a *colonia* and remained so for around 300 years. However, the ease with which she took Colchester so alarmed the Roman authorities, they built a wall around the town, the wall that can be seen today.

Colchester was later expanded using the original Roman road grid pattern. Excavations over the centuries have yielded a phantasmagoria of prizes – jewellery, skeletons, baths and a box flue. A Roman circus, the only one in Britain, was discovered in 2004 during excavations on the site of Colchester Garrison. Once the Romans left, Saxon raiding parties from Germany invaded. A few centuries later came the Normans, and during the 16th century, more Protestant martyrs were burnt alive here than in any other English town. No invaders have tried to take Colchester recently.

Address Balkerne Passage, Colchester, CO3 3AA | Getting there The gateway is about 400 yards north-west of Colchester Town station | Hours Accessible 24 hours | Tip In a small area of open space next to the police station stand the remains of what was probably a Romano-British church, one of the oldest of its kind in the country.

25 Uni of the Hard Left
Say you want a revolution

At the height of radical student activism in the 1960s and 1970s – the golden days of Wolfie Smith-styled protest, not the snowflakery of today – Essex University in Colchester was the place to go to for a Marxist-Leninist-Maoist dialectical punch-up.

Essex opened in 1964 as a plate-glass rather than red-brick university. Its aim was to break with tradition. The founders believed architecture should serve a social purpose and change society. So, typically for the time, the design was brutal and brutalist. The new university would be a 'vocational powerhouse to train a technocratic elite'. Instead of different buildings for different departments, everything was mixed. Blocks were distributed in a zig-zag to encourage students to meet those from different disciplines. Shockingly for the time, there was mixed-sex accommodation.

The students responded appreciatively. In-house revolutionaries included two of the leading extremists of the day, Angry Brigade members Hilary Creek and Anna Mendelssohn. Creek went to Paris to meet the French underground movement. The gendarmes then alleged she also collected 33 sticks of gelignite, later found in a Dalston flat. The obviously fascist judges gave her 10 years. In Holloway prison she became friends with Myra Hindley. Like Creek, Anna Mendelssohn also received a 10-year prison sentence at the Old Bailey in 1972: for conspiracy to cause explosions. At least David (now Lord) Triesman later only became general secretary of the sell-out Labour party.

It was not all doom and capitalist gloom. A speech by Enoch Powell was interrupted by a student dressed as Guy Fawkes brandishing a fake bomb (actually a grapefruit with a phoney fuse attached). Powell quickly made his exit and was chased off the campus by the student body. Colchester has recently been voted one of the 10 most political universities in the world. Ayes to the left.

Address Essex University, Wivenhoe Park, Colchester, CO4 3SQ, +44 (0)1206 873333, www.essex.ac.uk | Getting there The campus is just south of Clingoe Hill (the A 133), a mile south-east of Hythe station | Hours Accessible 24 hours – but remember that people live and work here | Tip Political turmoil was not invented in the 1960s. The Old Siege House Bar & Brasserie at 75 East Street was built in the late 15th century, and recalls the 1648 Siege of Colchester when a Royalist army was attacked by Parliamentarians and then laid siege for 11 weeks.

26_ The Witchfinder's Castle

Heads, you lose. Tales, he wins

Give thanks that you're living now in the safe and sensible 21st century, for 400 years ago in the 1640s, Essex was the witching county of Britain. More witches were executed here than anywhere else, with some 200 suspected women hanged. And it was in Colchester Castle, now a prime tourist attraction, that it happened, thanks to Matthew Hopkins, the notorious and self-proclaimed 'Witchfinder General'.

Hopkins was a lawyer but you wouldn't want him defending you; a parking charge might lead to the chair. He falsely claimed that Parliament during the English Civil War had appointed him to rid the area of witches. In the castle he imprisoned, interrogated and eliminated hundreds of women using sleep deprivation, forced standing and his main MO, which has since become part of the nation's shared psyche: suspected witches were 'swum' – tied up and thrown into water. If they sank, they had been hydraulically cleansed. If they floated, the water had rejected them and they had been guilty all along.

Many never made it to the water and died of jail fever in the castle cells. Many turned King's evidence – accusing others to get a lighter sentence. Maybe there was a financial element involved. Hopkins could earn the then enormous sum of £23 in Stowmarket, Suffolk, to condemn witches. With the greatest irony, Hopkins' lucrative career is believed to have come to an end after less than two years' de-witching when he himself was accused and 'swum'.

This was a time when suspicion and fear were intense, as the new Protestant strain of Christianity was unsettling the old certainties amid a lingering obsession with superstition and magic in a pre-scientific age. To get the best flavour of that period, nothing can beat Michael Reeves' aptly titled 1968 film *Witchfinder General*, one of the great cult classics, starring the inimitable Vincent Price as the ghastly Matthew Hopkins.

Address Colchester Castle, Ryegate Road, Colchester, CO1 1TJ, +44 (0)1206 282939, www.colchester.cimuseums.org.uk | Getting there The castle is 300 yards north of Colchester Town station, which itself is on the A 134 | Hours Mon–Sat 10am–5pm, Sun 11am–5pm | Tip Visit the castle itself to see some of the most significant Roman finds in Britain.

27 Constable Country
Most arresting views

John Constable is one of Britain's best loved painters. His works based on the gorgeous, gentle landscape by the River Stour, just north of Dedham, where Essex meets Suffolk, especially *The Hay Wain* from 1821, are seen by thousands in a host of galleries and have become a staple of place mats and pub prints.

Constable explained how exploring the area 'made me a painter and I am grateful. The sound of water escaping from mill dams, willows, old rotten planks, slimy posts, and brickwork, I love such things'. At the beginning of the 19th century, his paintings were the perfect romantic antidote to industrialisation. Yet he was mocked in England and only grudgingly elected to the Royal Academy, by just a single vote, when he was already into his fifties. Conversely, in France his work was embraced. They loved his brush work and the way he applied paint thickly with touches of white to create the effect of shimmering light.

Constable's explanations were formidable. 'The world is wide. No two days are alike, nor even two hours; neither were there ever two leaves of a tree alike since the creation of all the world.' There was also a political aspect to his work. The countryside was then under threat from the Enclosure Acts, which enabled landowners to fence off land and bar commoners.

Dedham is beautiful, particularly near the water meadows by the Stour, and with medieval buildings such as The Sun Inn, which retains its coaching arch, and black and white striped Southfields. It was a factory when Dedham was a wealthy wool town, and is now residential. The 15th-century church of St Mary the Virgin was the last medieval wool church to be built locally. Inside, on permanent display, is Constable's *The Ascension*. Ironically, Tom Keating, the famous art forger who trousered some £10 million for his reproductions, was a Dedham resident until his death in 1984.

Address North-east Essex, CO7 | Getting there Dedham is a little way east off the A 12, 7 miles from Colchester; train to Manningtree then a 25-minute walk | Tip Cross the border – no passport needed – into nearby Suffolk to visit Willy Lott's Cottage, as featured in the renowned *The Hay Wain*.

28 __ Crashed Plane Memorial

It's got its nose to the ground

No, it's not a crashed plane whose nose was embedded into the ground as it made a forced landing. It's a sculpture of the same, its tail in the air, set on an elevated stone platform.

The model is not a Spitfire, as many think, but a De Havilland Mosquito, the unusual war-time aircraft made mostly of wood. The sculpture is located here, a mile from the centre of Bradwell-on-Sea, because the site was an airfield during World War II and the RAF wanted the memorial to honour the 121 people who died on war-time missions that began at this airfield. Unfortunately, the memorial plaques around the sculpture have some mistakes – misspelled names, ranks and countries, the alphabetical order jumbled up.

Bradwell was the only fighter airfield fitted with FIDO, a faithful system that cleared fog away from the runway by burning thousands of gallons of petrol. Fog was a recurring problem on account of the airfield's isolated marshland position on the Dengie Peninsula.

Aircraft from Bradwell supported the 1944 D-Day invasions, providing air cover over the English Channel, and intercepted V-1 flying bombs when pilots skilfully tipped them off course using wing contact. Bradwell closed at the end of the war; nevertheless, its remains are all around. The Control Tower is a private house and parts of the runway can still be seen.

In the undergrowth there are air-raid shelters, an anti-tank block in the bushes, overgrown hangers, some Nissen huts and even the battle headquarters hidden in a hedgerow. Some of the FIDO oil burners are still around and have even been used as plant pots.

In the Dengie nature reserve beyond there are pillboxes: concrete blockhouses that were used as defence stations. To the north, to add to the debris, albeit on a much larger scale, is the hulk of Bradwell nuclear power station, the first such to be decommissioned. Perhaps all the uranium has half-lifed into lead.

Address 9 Trusses Road, Bradwell-on-Sea, CM0 7QS | Getting there The memorial is half-way between the village and the old nuclear power station | Hours Accessible 24 hours | Tip Such is the stark beauty of the peninsula, nearby is the Saltmarsh Coastal Trail, which spans 75 miles of stunning local coastline in the county that has the most in England.

29 Lonely Church by the Sea
On this wall I will build my church

Strikingly placed on the windswept coast in the remotest of locations is the remarkable survival that is the church of St Peter-on-the-Wall. It's the church closest to the sea in Britain and one of the oldest intact places of worship in the country, dating back to the year A.D. 654, and still in use. There aren't exactly many potential worshippers to make up the congregation, and so members from the local utopian Othona Christian Community do their best.

The earliest local history dates back to the third century when the Romans built a fort nearby at the most easterly part of the Dengie Peninsula and on the south side of the Blackwater Estuary. This was a most strategic position; they could now control access to the Black-water and Colne Rivers, the latter leading to their main base, Col-chester, one of the most important cities in Roman Britain.

In the year A.D. 653, King Sigeberht the Good travelled south from Lindisfarne to spread Christianity. By then the Roman fort was in ruins and Bishop Cedd decided the spot was perfect for a church for the East Saxons. Now locals could pray to God that the weather and the winds wouldn't destroy their community. The chapel was dedicated to Saint Peter, the first Bishop of Rome – that is the first Pope – the name Peter coming from the Greek *petra*, rock, to whom Jesus said: 'Upon this rock I will build my church'. Bishop Cedd's chapel, built using Roman bricks and stones, was next to the abandoned Roman wall, hence the chapel's name, St Peter-on-the-Wall.

Records of its later use are sparse. In 1442, the local clergy reported to the Bishop of London that it had been burnt down, but it was later used as a barn, and in 1920 restored and re-consecrated. St Peter now belongs to Chelmsford Cathedral. The adjacent field is used during the annual Bradwell Pilgrimage, held on the first Saturday in July.

Address East End Road, Bradwell-on-Sea, CM0 7PN, +44 (0)1621 776846, www.bradwellchapel.org | **Getting there** Take the B 1021 east along the River Blackwater towards Bradwell-on-Sea and continue east | **Hours** Open occasionally, at normal service times – visit website to check details of possible visits | **Tip** Head east to the sea and the Othona Christian Community set up after World War II by RAF chaplain Norman Motley as a place for people of all faiths and none to find reconciliation and renewal.

30 _ Petrified Forest at Furze

It's coming, it's in the trees!

They say it's the loneliest place on Earth; well, all right, in Essex. It's not just lonely and remote, it's weird and other worldly. It's the Dengie Peninsula. No surprise that this wild, wind-swept waste was the inspiration for where the Martians landed in H. G. Wells' *War of the Worlds*.

Of all the strange sights here, little can beat the petrified forest of rotten oak and ash in the Furze, a rare surviving local copse, the last section of what was once a huge ancient woodland that was used to build the royal fleet. Now the twisted, tortured trees appear spookily out of the marshy mist like something from a Wes Craven horror film. They look dangerous, the edginess borne out of the desolate surrounds. Many people have seen faces in the trees. One saw a general ordering his troops to attack, another three friends gathered around a campfire telling stories, one of the stumps screaming. There's the tree that supposedly has red eyes and a mad stare, and one split by lightning into a two-headed calf.

How perfect that many of the trees are oaks. The oak, the king of the forest, has always been associated with the supreme gods such as Zeus or Thor, with power over thunder and lightning. Druids worshipped in oak groves; indeed the word 'druid' itself might have come from a Celtic word meaning 'knower of the oak tree'. The magical mistletoe often grows on oaks, and kings wore crowns of oak to prove their status as its king on Earth.

The other dominant tree in Furze is the ash. The tree was sacred to the Vikings, whose gods made magical spears of ash wood. To the Anglo-Saxons, the Vikings were known as 'Aescling' – men of ash – who in folklore were said to have healing powers. Don't try this at home, but newborn babes were given a teaspoon of ash sap and sick children would be passed naked through a cleft in the ash to cure them. Well, what can you do if there's no booster jab available?!

Address Mundon, Maldon, CM9 6PA | **Getting there** Head to Maldon and take Fambridge Road, the B 1010, south | **Hours** Viewable from a public footpath | **Tip** Head for St Mary's Church in nearby Mundon, so ignored its future has been taken on by the group Friends of Friendless Churches.

31 Crass' Country Commune
How does it feel...?

Leave the rat race, the workaday world, worries about a mortgage, job, status, rising energy bills, the last bus home and get it together in the country, well, Epping Forest, about as wild as it gets in the soft south, at Dial House farm cottage in Ongar Great Park.

Dial House has been a sustainable anarcho-pacifist (don't say hippie) open house since 1967. It is also the long-time home of Crass, the legendary anarcho-punk band. Crass came of age in the late 1970s when a music revolution saw scores of bands appear in the wake of those punk trendsetters the Sex Pistols and the Clash. Many adopted a DIY anti-establishment ethos but few were as politically motivated as Crass. In 1982 they released 'How Does It Feel To Be The Mother Of 1,000 Dead?', a denunciation of then PM Margaret Thatcher and her Falklands War, which made the Sex Pistols' 'Anarchy in the UK' seem like a Bee Gees ballad.

The ruling Conservative Party even considered suing the band. Robin Eggar of the *Daily Mirror* claimed Crass had gone too far with what he called 'the most revolting and unnecessary record I have ever heard'. But then, his brother was a Tory MP. The Public Prosecutor had a long look and decided 'nothing to see here, move on', or legal words to that effect.

Dial House is a large, rambling 16th-century farm cottage. In the 1960s, artist, writer and philosopher Penny Rimbaud – not the name known to his mum – began work on restoring the property. It was he who founded Crass, and Dial House soon became a haven for bohemian spirits and avant-garde creative types outside the system promoting projects such as the Stonehenge Free Festival, that's when the organisers were not being chased for drugs busts, served with eviction notices, or patronised by local shopkeepers as 'the students'. Current plans are for a 'Centre for the Radical Arts'; that's if The Man doesn't get here first.

Address Dial House, North Weald Bassett, Epping, CM16 6GQ | **Getting there** Take the A 414 to its junction with the B 181, head south for a short stretch and then trek through the woods | **Hours** By arrangement – you'll have to contact them by post | **Tip** Want to make a quick getaway? A short distance west is North Weald Airfield, which opened in 1916 to combat Zeppelin raids. That's Zeppelin *air* raids, not Led Zeppelin.

32 _ Cricket on Top of the M25
Just don't hit a six

The perfect Sunday summer setting. The sound of willow on leather, striped coloured caps, expertly creased whites, the umpire stuffed with pullovers, pleas of 'Howzat?'. What could be better than afternoon cricket with only half an hour to go before tea and cucumber sandwiches? Just the bother of the world's most roaring and noise-filled motorway underneath the pitch! Yes, Epping Foresters Cricket Club play at Mill Plain on top of the orbital M25, rather than on a village green by a sleepy church in the heart of the countryside.

There's no catch. The cricket club came first. It was founded in 1947 by a group of ex-servicemen who negotiated with the Epping Forest conservators to take up what was swampy land and had to be drained before they could launch their first innings. When, 30 years later, the authorities announced that a new super-road would bulldoze through the boundaries, there was only one test for the Epping Foresters – to hit the highway hustlers for six. Instead of the club moving to fresh pastures, they stayed and the motorway moved – underneath the cricket pitch. At enormous cost, the Bell Common Tunnel was built for 500 yards between junctions 26 and 27 from 1982 to 1984. The club nevertheless had to relocate for five years before resuming its original position.

Motorists wondering whether a strong stray stroke might smash their windscreen can drive safely: the pitch is at some distance from the edge of the tunnel roof. Not even Garry Sobers could hit that far. The club plays in the Herts & Essex League, and there are also age-group teams for children and a Sunday league for casual players. The club has announced that 'everyone is welcome to bring a deckchair and watch cricket for nothing in this lovely green open space above London's busiest motorway'. At least the corridor of uncertainty has been resolved.

Address High Road Epping, CM16 4DL, +44 (0)1992 579700, www.eppingforesterscc.play-cricket.com | Getting there High Road Epping is the B 1393; Epping tube station is a mile to the east | Hours Check website for match days and times | Tip Don't fancy cricket? There's always Epping Town Football Club who play in Division One of the Essex Olympian League, ground sharing with Epping Upper Clapton Rugby Football Club in the Thornwood area of the forest.

33__The Gilwell Oak

Be prepared for this scouts' honour of a tree

Majestic, magnificent, marvellous, the Gilwell Oak is no ordinary tree. Not only was it allegedly used by Dick Turpin as a hideaway (among several hundred other trees), where he would wait for stage coaches, but it was voted Tree of the Year by the public in 2017, beating a large field thanks to votes from many branches. The great tree is technically the Common or English Oak, *Quercus robur*, and is around 500 years old. It can be found in the grounds of the Scout Association's headquarters at Gilwell Park, just north of Chingford.

Scouting began in 1907 when Baden-Powell hosted a boys' camp on Brownsea Island, Dorset. Boys from different social backgrounds participated in such activities as observation, woodcraft, chivalry, lifesaving and patriotism. The Scout Association bought the land in 1919 and it has enjoyed many connections with scouting. This is where the first Scout leaders trained in the early years of the 20th century. Its wood was used for badges, although nowadays the badges are made from alternative materials, but special commemorative beads carved from the Gilwell Oak are sold by The Scout Association to its leaders. The oak even inspired scout founder Robert Baden-Powell's 1929 slogan about the movement creating 'the moral of the acorn and the oak'. This held that 'big things were possible from modest beginnings', and so the Scouts would grow just like the oak from humble acorn to mighty tree.

Nowadays the chief scout is Bear Grylls, and he has explained how 'the Gilwell Oak has been the backdrop to hundreds of courses in which thousands of volunteer leaders have been inspired and motivated to change young people's lives. It's the unbending symbol of Scouting's desire to change the world for the better'. Scouts nowadays come from all over to see the great oak and take a leaf or acorn as a souvenir of their visit.

Address Waltham Abbey, E 4 7QW, www.scouts.org.uk | **Getting there** The Gilwell Oak is in Gilwell Park, half-way between the huge reservoir and West Essex Golf Club; take Bury Road north from Chingford | **Hours** By arrangement with the Scouts; visit the website or email heritage@scouts.org.uk to book a place on a tour | **Tip** Head south down Bury Road towards Chingford and Queen Elizabeth's Hunting Lodge, built by her father, Henry VIII, as a lookout for chasing deer.

34 Pole Hill Meridian Marker

It divides the country, not just the forest

This is not just any old granite obelisk. This is a marker with a serious story behind it. Pole Hill obelisk lies at latitude 51 degrees 38 minutes north, but more importantly right on the 0 degrees Meridian longitude. From the top there are extensive views over London when the trees are not in full bloom.

The obelisk is also at the Meridian's highest point in Britain, 100 yards above sea level. This meant it could be used as a marker by geographers at the Greenwich Observatory to set their telescopes and achieve a true zero degree bearing. Pole Hill obelisk also has a little brother alongside, while the main man bears the inscription:

This pillar was erected in 1824 under the direction of the Reverend John Pond, MA, Astronomer Royal. It was placed on the Greenwich Meridian and its purpose was to indicate the direction of true north from the transit telescope of the Royal Observatory.

The very position of the Meridian has caused much controversy. Originally, as far as Britain was concerned, it went through Richmond, south-west London, and the King's observatory at Kew. Later, the authorities decided to move it to Greenwich because it was in the observatory there that John Harrison devised the first ever means of calculating the time at sea. It took an international conference in Washington in 1884 for the world to agree that 0 degrees should go through London and Greenwich – that is the world other than France, who wanted it to go through Paris, natch. In the end, an agreement was reached. London would win as long as Britain immediately adopted the metric system, something that still hasn't happened properly 150 years later.

When the weather is right it is possible to see from Pole Hill the Laser at Greenwich marking the Meridian.

Address Woodberry Way, Chingford, E 4 7DX | **Getting there** The obelisk is a short distance north of the A 110 and about a mile west of Chingford railway station | **Hours** Accessible 24 hours | **Tip** An inscription on the obelisk reveals the local connections with the legendary T. E. Lawrence, the Great War military hero. Lawrence bought much of the local land and built a hut to install a printing press. It was later demolished and rebuilt at the nearby property The Warren, Loughton, home of the City of London authority that runs Epping Forest.

35 — Woody Den for the Famous
And it's good old country comfort

Wood House in deepest Epping Forest likes its famous residents. During World War II, none other than Winston Churchill used it as a foresty bolthole miles away from Whitehall. In recent years it has been occupied by the inimitable song stylist Sir Roderick of Stewart and lately occasional footballer Andy Carroll.

Palladian-styled Wood House was built in 1895. In the mid-1980s Rod Stewart moved in and lived there for 30 years with the odd wife and girlfriend, or two. He would invite players from Newcastle United, Liverpool and his favourite team Celtic to train on its full-sized football pitch. In 2016, Stewart put The Wood House on the market for £7.5 million. Amazingly there were no takers, despite the property's grand 45-foot reception hall, early 15th-century stone fireplace, 6 bedrooms, 11 bathrooms, tennis courts, boating lake, swimming pool and Eden-style gardens.

According to his latest wife, Penny Lancaster, 'Rod and I found ourselves affected by the recent property stalemate thanks to' – wait for it – 'Brexit', without mentioning that the excessive price might be a factor. Eventually, Rod realised the first price cut would be the deepest and took a £3.4 million hit, selling the mansion for £4.1 million to Andy Carroll (as many as 33 goals in 126 games as the main striker for West Ham).

Carroll moved in with fiancée Billi Mucklow, star of *The Only Way Is Essex*, the unwatchable, vapid reality TV show. Essex society was agog at the thought of Carroll installing his usual zebra-print wallpaper and a mirrored ceiling. Later pictures taken from inside the property, now dubbed 'Carroll Castle', reveal pink satin sofas and animal print cushions alongside Miss Mucklow's beauty salon, 'Billutifuls'. Highlight is a Snow White mirror with the words 'mirror, mirror on the wall' written in pink lights so that Andy Carroll can watch himself score.

Address Wood House, Epping Forest, CM16 5HT | Getting there Up a long track off High Road (B 1393) | Hours Best not to disturb Andy Carroll really | Tip Rod has since moved to 10-bedroom £5 million Durrington House just east of Harlow, which features an 18th-century clock tower.

36 — Billy Bragg's A13
Route 666

Forget the A1 and the Yellow Brick Road. Where the USA has Route 66, Essex has the A13, often more like Route 666, the devil's playground, in the form of hairy, lairy, scary bikers tonning it up past Gallows' Corner to stop for a shoshij shamwij at a Little Chef, or for some greasy Castrol GTX at Sid's Garage.

To Billy Bragg, the Bard of Barking, the estuarian essayist of Essex, the A13 arterial route out of east London is the road of dreams – dreams of Coryton, the tiny town made of oil, dreams of potted shrimps in Old Leigh, dreams of an evening at the rock 'n' roll repository that was the Kursaal and nightmares of waking up dodging the big navy guns on Foulness Island. Bragg's song, 'A13, Trunk Road to the Sea', mimics Bobby Troup's American paean, 'Route 66', made famous by the Rolling Stones. More esoteric, but in keeping with the myth of the road, is a spoken word track simply called 'A13' by bass monster Jah Wobble in which he lambasts the 'hopeless highway of Essex'.

You know the A13 is taking you into deepest Essex when as the road crosses the River Lea, the historic border between London and Essex, there's an exciting TOTSO – a turn-off to stay on – followed by some heartwarming sights: a new flyover at Beckton Alps; the dying Ford works at Dagenham; the Litmus Towers near Rainham whose LED arrays display environmental data; the Dartford Crossing, the highest on the Thames; until the end is nigh on the approach to the great capital of Essex: Southend.

The A13 does funny things to people. In February 2016 a disgruntled construction worker stole his boss' truck and drove for 40 miles along the road, bumping into various objects including police vehicles. Only on the A13 could a Coca-Cola lorry crash – no casualties – leading to a can-full of jokes on social media along the lines of 'I'd like to buy the world an 11-mile traffic jam'.

Address All the way from Central London to south Essex | **Tip** Don't fancy the A13? Try its more northerly brother, the A12, better known as the thunderous, never-stopping Eastern Avenue, whose expansion has cut a swathe through the communities it divides in its path as it reaches out through Essex into Suffolk.

37 Peasants' Revolt Memorial
Wat a time to march on London

It's one of the most infamous protest marches in British history. Even the most bored schoolchild has heard of the Peasants' Revolt of 1381. But few would know that it began in this tiny Essex village.

Trouble began when the locals, already suffering from the Black Death, were shocked to discover a government man in their midst wondering why the villagers hadn't paid their poll tax. The bill was three groats per person, no matter how much a person owned, and had been introduced to fund the country's overseas interests.

The villagers took exception and threw him out. However, the Fobbing poll tax collectors got off lightly. In Brentwood, their party was attacked violently and six officials killed. Then the mysterious Wat Tyler joined in as one of the main protestors. Was he born in Brenchley, Kent, or somewhere in Essex? Two more Essex men appeared with similar leadership qualities. John Ball was a priest enthusiastic about 'Lollardy', the new anti-establishment Christianity instigated by John Wycliffe who wanted people to be able to read the Bible in English. Jack Straw might also have been a preacher. He turned rebel after a tax collector assaulted his daughter, went under the alias of John Tyler, and is even believed by some historians to have been Wat Tyler himself.

Eventually, Tyler, John Ball and Jack Straw (no relation to the late 20th-century Labour home secretary), whoever they were, set off for London with their grievances. In the capital they caused mayhem. Although they met the King, Richard II, they also met with a bloody end.

Wat Tyler was stabbed by one of the King's squires. John Ball was hanged, drawn and quartered, Jack Straw was executed and his head displayed on London Bridge. The poll tax was abolished for just 600 years. Fittingly, this memorial, by Ben Coode-Adams, was erected to commemorate the 600th anniversary in 1981.

The Strong Shall Help the Weak

Address High Road, Fobbing, SS 17 9JD | **Getting there** By car, take the A 176 south from the A 13 at the Murco petrol station | **Hours** Accessible 24 hours | **Tip** The Peasants' Revolt was probably planned at Fobbing's 14th-century White Lion pub on Lion Hill, which was then a chandler's, where sails were made.

38_ The Broomway
Britain's deadliest path

Enter at your peril! The Broomway has long been described as Britain's deadliest path, nicknamed the Doomway, and has claimed hundreds of lives over the years. As for the Ordnance Survey, few other rights of way disappear twice a day, and so the map of this area prints in large pink letters: *Rights of Way across Maplin Sands can be dangerous. Seek local guidance.*

To add to the peril there are mud traps and worse, quicksand, and to worry visitors further, signs indemnify the MOD against drownings, explosions and mud deaths. Just to add to the frisson of fear, there are also signs that warn: *Do not approach or touch any object as it may explode and kill you.* Other than that, everything's fine.

So why the problem? The Broomway crosses vast mud flats that stretch for miles along the unsloped land in one of the lowest settings in the country.

When the tide goes out on Foulness Island, it goes out absurdly far, and the underfoot is packed so hard it tempts the trekker like a sandy siren. Then, alas, the tide returns, spreading itself across the land and sand quicker than a man can run or a horse gallop, as locals say, especially if the weather gets a bit hairy.

The name Broomway comes from the brooms that used to be placed on either side of the track to aid safe passage. Before 1932, the Broomway was the only means of access to and from Foulness, other than by boat, for Foulness Island is separated from the mainland by crafty creeks and mud stretches. Locals say that if you arrive at Wakering Stairs, to the west of Foulness, for the start of the path and it's a misty day, not to proceed.

Foulness Island has been run by the Ministry of Defence since World War I, when they took control to monitor potential German invaders, and they've never left. The MOD that is, not the Germans. Artillery tests are carried out with plenty of prior warning.

Address Foulness Island, SS3 9XT | Getting there It's best to find an OS map and walk. The only access to Foulness Island by road is at Landwick police lodge, a mile from Great Wakering. Residents are issued with permits that they must show to security guards when entering the restricted MOD zone. | Hours You have been warned! | Tip If you have the stamina and rations, and better still a boat, a most rewarding and unusual day can be spent exploring the inlets and creeks around the Rivers Crouch and Roach, and the Bridgemarsh Creek.

39__Fancy Frinton Beach Huts
So posh even the dog poo smells sweet

Tree-lined avenues sweep down to the elegant, exclusive esplanade. Men in plus-fours gather gallantly around the greensward. Ladies with parasols parade primly along the promenade.

No, it's not a P. G. Wodehouse film set, it's fancy Frinton, in the sun as magnificent as Miami, as posh as Palm Beach. Some call it snooty, some call it superior, some say the noses are all made of toffee. Yes, Frinton retains an atmosphere of the 1920s. The beach is quiet and secluded, and filled with gaily coloured beach huts given such names as St Ronan's, The Poplars and Actæon. It's hard to believe that gruesome Jaywick (see ch. 22) is only a few miles down the coast.

In the 1890s, Frinton failed to make the Baedeker Guide, so Sir Richard Powell Cooper dreamt up plans for a high-class resort. But there were to be strict rules: no sea-front amusements, no pier, no shorts at the golf club and no pubs. Frinton became a haunt for the rich and famous. Prime Minister David Lloyd-George rented a furnished house. The Court Circular from *The Times* revealed a list of lords and ladies spending a large part of their summer at Frinton in that pre-foreign holidays era. There was yachting and an annual tennis tournament. Securing a hut was at a premium but vital for lounging around in striped dressing gowns before donning a one-piece swim suit for a bit of Esther Williams. Frinton remained exclusive. As recently as 1984 the council was still banning the sale of fresh fish on the beach.

As for those huts, radio presenter James Max bought one for £28,000 in 2018. 'It leaked, had a peeling paint job and was musty inside. But it is absolutely one of my best purchasing decisions.' Recently there have been dramas. In 2006, the town lost its battle to keep the 'Frinton Gates' – a level-crossing barrier that divided the posh side from the posher side. And now a pub has opened. It's the end of civilisation.

Address Frinton-on-Sea, CO13 | Getting there The beach is at the southern end of the B 1033; train to Frinton-on-Sea | Hours Accessible 24 hours | Tip Head to Connaught Avenue, the 'Bond Street' of East Anglia, for the most stylish shops on this coast.

40 — Sunshine Homes by the Sea
Utopia nearly realised

Some of the world's greatest between-the-wars architects came to Frinton in the early years of the 20th century to build heavenly havens and houses for the handsomely rich. It was all part of the Frinton Park project, the largest group of individually designed Modernist houses in the country. The scheme was lorded over by the masterly Oliver Hill, he of Midland Hotel Morecambe fame, who came back from Monte Carlo enthused.

Frinton Park was launched in 1934 with Hill's Round House, a show home and information centre for the project that featured a mosaic on the dining room floor illustrating the entire plan for the grand estate. Oliver Hill built gorgeous houses on Audley Way, 'Dawn' and 'Sunnyholme', which were featured in the original sales brochure and pictured in a 1935 *Country Life* article 'A Planned Seaside Resort'. Initially, 1,000 Art Deco houses were planned, alongside a shopping centre, hotel and town hall. All to be built in the then experimental material, concrete.

To share his dream, Hill invited several young, idealistic and progressive architects: Wells Coates, best known for the utopian Isokon in Hampstead; Maxwell Fry, who designed the influential Sun House, also in Hampstead; and the Erich Mendelsohn-Serge Chermayeff partnership responsible for the famed De La Warr Pavilion in Bexhill.

Sadly, despite the lofty ideals, few of the planned houses were built. The public was simply not attuned to the latest architectural ideas. Reactionary building societies refused to fund concrete structures. Old hat bricks and mortar were used instead, which discouraged the purist new wave architects from committing themselves. Only 40 homes were built and the company behind the scheme collapsed in 1936. Of the 40 houses built, only 15 remain. Damned traditionalists.

Address A useful guide produced by Radical Essex plots all the houses: www.radicalessex.uk/wp-content/uploads/2017/06/Frinton-Park-Estate-Walking-Tour.pdf | Getting there Audley Way is half way between Tendring Technology College and the sea, and also half way between Frinton and Walton-on-the-Naze stations | Hours Accessible 24 hours | Tip Out to sea is a huge windfarm, but it's on Gunfleet Sands, a treacherous sandbank that has caused hundreds of shipwrecks.

41 The Council House Palace

In Xanadu did Kubla Khan a stately pleasure dome…

It's billed as 'Britain's most extraordinary house'. No, not the one in which Boris Johnson has his shirt tucked in and combs his hair, or the abode where the Gallagher brothers serve orange pekoe tea in little china cups to maiden aunts. It's Talliston House & Gardens, a former council house just a few miles from Stansted Airport, which has been turned into a bizarre, timeless, surrealist psyche-delic experience.

It all began in 1990 when journalist and author John Trevillian bought the property. Working with a team of artists, volunteers and tradesmen, he began to transform it into a 'labyrinth of locations from different times and places', rebuilding it over 25 years into a fantasy palace with nearly 2,000 antiques dotted around.

The 13 separate locations recreate eras dating back to 4000 B.C., on to today, and forward to A.D. 2228. Trevillian began with a room based on a 1930s film noir theme and has since added a Moorish bed-chamber, a Victorian tower, and a kitchen where everything, even the cutlery, is entirely derived from and devoted to 1950s New Orleans. There's a 1920s New York-style office, a Japanese conservatory, and a flight of stairs straight out of a fairytale castle. The Hall of Mirrors is inspired by Italy's ghost villages, the Cabin takes you to Whiskey Jack's wooden warren in the windswept wilds of Canada, while Eish Al Kamar (Arabic for 'moon's nest') is the Room of Dreams based on the original military fortress of the Alhambra.

In 2014 it looked like Trevillian would have to sell, despite spend-ing more than £500,000 on his magical project, but public outcry led to substantial donations that allowed him to stay. It was opened to the public in October 2015, exactly 25 years after work began. Tre-villian now explains that all proceeds go to maintaining the prop-erty. 'Each room has its own smells, sounds, candles. Costly things to upkeep.'

Address Talliston, Newton Green, Great Dunmow, CM6 1DU, +44 (0)7760 171100,
www.talliston.com | Getting there Talliston is four miles east of Stansted Airport, just north
of the A 120 | Hours Visit the website for details of house and garden tours, events, dining
and B&B | Tip Continuing the *outré* artefacts is the Angels Wine Tower in the Radisson
Blu Hotel at Stansted Airport, which displays more than 4,000 bottles of wine in a soaring
glass case. If you order a bottle that's not within reach, an attendant, or 'angel', is hoisted in
the air to extract it.

42 — Royalty's Abandoned Fort
Castle near the sand

You can see why ancient kings and queens wanted a castle here at one of the south-eastern ends of the country: they could make a quick getaway back to France where they had regal links and often assumed the possibility of taking part in some conquering.

Most of Hadleigh Castle, located a few miles west of Southend, has long withered away, but it is still a fascinating site for a spot of medieval-themed exploration. In 1215, King John gave the land, prime hunting ground on one side, marshland on the other, to Hubert de Burgh, Justiciar of England and Earl of Kent, and custodian of strategic castles at Windsor and Dover. Unfortunately, Hubert himself fell from grace soon after construction began. He was imprisoned and had his castle seized by the Crown. Worse still, the large turreted castle he had built was situated on what was unstable clay. By 1274, folk were moaning that it was 'badly built and decayed' and land slips then saw parts of the castle collapse. Nevertheless, the 14th-century king, Edward III, spent money on a new gateway and high tower, surrounding the castle with parkland and an orchard. After all, Hadleigh was strategically important, guarding the Thames Estuary and the approach to London, which was why kings continued to spend money on its upkeep.

Hadleigh remained a crown castle for 200 years and was traditionally passed to the king's consort as part of her wedding dowry. This happened to three of Henry VIII's wives – Catherine of Aragon, Anne of Cleves and Catherine Parr. It all changed after Henry's death. His son, Edward VI, sold the castle to Lord Riche, who plundered the building for stone. It then fell into disuse, disrepair and ruin. Some of the 14th-century round towers remain, as well as pieces of the curtain wall. The site is very popular with walkers and picnickers, with wonderful views to the strange lands of Canvey Island.

Address Castle Lane, Hadleigh, Benfleet, SS 7 2AP, +44 (0)370 3331181, www.english-heritage.org.uk | Getting there Train to Leigh-on-Sea, then a 1.5-mile walk; by car, take the A 13 to the junction with Castle Lane and head south | Hours Accessible 24 hours | Tip Where better than the Castle pub in Hadleigh itself after all that medieval exploring?

43_ The Salvation Army Farm
'Salvation à la mode and a cup of tea'

Here on the outskirts of Southend, in estuarian woodland, the Salvation Army's Hadleigh Farm carries on the work of the Victorian founder, William Booth, and the organisation's core mission: 'Love God, Love Others'. Booth set up the Hadleigh Farm in 1891 to take the homeless and unemployed away from the horrors of Whitechapel and pubs full of 'blaspheming infidels and boisterous drunkards'.

Here, in Hadleigh, the Salvation Army taught farming and brick-making as part of a hand-up out of poverty, rather than a hand-out. Their successors now run the place as a haven for rare breeds – beasties that you wouldn't necessarily meet in yer average Sunday afternoon park. Try the Bagot goats for instance. They were brought to England by returning Crusaders and gifted to John Bagot of Blithfield by Richard II after a fine afternoon's hunting. No lawnmower? One of these will clear your patch as a starter before lunch.

The Leicester Longwools are seriously hairy sheep that don't like the rain. Not as sturdy as the Greyface Dartmoor who have been munching their way across the sparse expanse since prehistoric times. Middle White pigs will never win an animalian beauty contest. Originally, they were known as London Porkers, from the days when everyone in the capital, apart from devout Jews, ate the flesh of the pig and vegetarianism had not yet been invented by Morrissey.

The Exmoor pony is a bit bigger. They're the cousins of the ones that still roam semi-wild on the Devon moorland, cleverly managing conservation. Thank God there are no foxes in the vicinity because the farm also contains Marsh Daisy chickens, which love to forage for food, and Derbyshire Redcap chickens, named after their unusually large comb. The Buff Orpingtons are placid, friendly and docile. They can even be handled. Just don't tell the Pied / Crollwitzer turkeys when it's coming up to Christmas.

Address Castle Lane, Hadleigh, Benfleet, SS 7 2AP, +44 (0)1702 426260, www.hadleighfarm.org.uk | **Getting there** Train to Leigh-on-Sea or Benfleet, then a short bus ride; by car, take the A 13 to the junction with Castle Lane and head south | **Hours** Visit website for details of special events; Rare Breeds Centre daily 10am–3.30pm, Hub Café in Chapel Lane daily 9.30am–4.30pm | **Tip** This is an area mostly reclaimed by nature, but for more typical touristy fare, head into nearby Canvey Island for the Castle Point Transport Museum.

44 Harlow – Sculpture Town

Where the whole town is a museum of stone

No town in Britain is as devoted to sculpture – modern, avant-garde – as Harlow New Town. When Harlow was being devised in the late 1940s, it was at a time when enlightened civil servants were determined that experimental new ways of living should go hand-in-hand, brush-in-brush, with high-quality art. Nothing was too good for ordinary working folk, or as a council official noted 'Sculpture is part of the fabric of everyday life within the town.'

This was no idle boast, for there are 90 works dotted around the town including pieces by some of the greatest artists imaginable, such as Auguste Rodin, Henry Moore and Barbara Hepworth. In charge was architect Frederick Gibberd who at the same time was designing new terminal buildings for Heathrow Airport.

Gibberd was inspired by trips to Florence. Walking through the Piazza della Signoria in that great Italian city and looking at Michelangelo's *David*, he saw sculpture as a way of giving a place identity. He called Harlow 'the Florence of Essex'. In 1953, Gibberd set up the Harlow Art Trust to acquire the sculptures. Money came from grants, corporate sponsorships and other resources. Harlow's first sculpture was Barbara Hepworth's *Contrapuntal Forms*, now based in a quiet housing estate. A year later, Henry Moore's *Family Group* arrived outside the Harlow Playhouse. Finn Thomson later came up with a set of three benches and a plaque titled *Moore Waiting Room* next to it. The town's Rodin sculpture is in the Water Gardens outside Nando's, while *Boar* (1957) is by Elizabeth Frink, whose work was shaped by three themes: the nature of Man, the horsieness of horses, and the divine in human form.

Harlow continued to commission new artefacts and work with art students. It was this approach that resulted in Ralph Brown's *Sheep Shearer* in 1956 and his *Meat Porters* for the Market Square in 1959. Harlow became the world's first Sculpture Town in 2010.

Address Throughout the town – check www.sculpturetown.uk for a map that shows all the locations and suggests interesting trails | Hours Most of the sculptures are outdoors, so accessible 24 hours. Check the website for the opening hours of indoor venues. | Tip The Henry Moore Archive has images, videos, letters and books that tell the story of how Harlow developed.

45 The Lawn
Britain's first residential tower block

Into the exciting, aspirational, hope-filled, post-war Britain came a new phenomenon, the tower block. Streets in the sky reaching to the heavens. Close, comfortable communities with stunning views and inside toilets. Up they went, tower after tower, block after block.

It was all down to the mightily influential writings of the 20th-century's leading architect, Charles-Édouard Jeanneret, better known as Le Corbusier. When asked by a group of city officials about urban design, he replied: 'Fine, I shall design a great fountain and behind it place a city for three million people.' Town planners lapped up Le Corbusier's ideas, resulting among other delights in this, The Lawn, the first residential tower block in the country to leap off the architectural drawings.

Built on the outskirts of Old Harlow, its opening in 1951 coincided with the Festival of Britain. The Lawn was designed by Frederick Gibberd, master planner for Harlow New Town, also responsible for the first three Heathrow terminals. Gibberd deployed a butterfly design for the four flats on each floor, each balcony and living room facing south. On the ground was the first ever pedestrian precinct. Upon completion, The Lawn was awarded a Ministry of Health Housing medal.

Within 25 years there were 440,000 flats in high-rise buildings in Britain, the number voraciously boosted by government subsidies for every storey added. But by then people realised that away from the council committees and their lofty utopian ideals, living above the first floor soon palled. The lifts kept on breaking down and weren't mended quickly, and just one up-to-no-goodnik family letting their dog poo on the corridors and their kids play the latest record at full blast brought down the tone of the whole block, while feelings of separation, isolation and seclusion soon overcame many inhabitants. Utopia became dystopia.

Address Off Mark Hall Moors, Harlow, CM20 2JX | Getting there The tower is just west of the A 414 and half a mile south of Harlow Mill station | Hours Accessible 24 hours | Tip Head for the Gibberd Garden on Marsh Lane CM17 0NA, designed by and dedicated to Mr Harlow himself, with its formal lawns, streams and glades, artefacts, sculptures and moated castle.

46 Anti-Invasion Fort

They fought long to save the fortress and the port

Harwich has always been one of Britain's greatest ports and therefore had to be powerfully defended. This was the answer: the Redoubt Fort, a circular defence structure built in 1808 on a hilltop by the estuaries of the Rivers Orwell and the Stour, at the entrance to the harbour, to defend this strategic site against invasion from Napoleon's finest. It supported Landguard Fort, on the opposite shore near Felixstowe, and, as part of the scheme, a further 28 Martello Towers were erected on the east coast.

The fort is made of brick with stone dressings. It is 200 feet in diameter with a central parade ground 85 feet across. There are still 10 guns on the battlements. Below, 18 casements were built to house 300 troops if a siege was on. These casements were used for accommodation, stores, toilets and a cookhouse. A regiment was on hand equipped with sufficient food and stores.

The Redoubt was originally armed with 10 24-pounder cannons. In the 1860s, the fort was reinforced with 68-pounders to withstand enemy artillery. It was used during World War II as an anti-aircraft site and even as a detention centre for British troops awaiting trial. Some of their graffiti remains. Yet no shot was ever fired from the fort and no enemy directly challenged it. But, sadly, a serious non-military problem took place locally in 1953. The horrendous Essex floods hit the surrounding land, which was below sea level, and eight lives were lost.

With modern day warfare taking on new technology, and the EU unlikely to send gunboats across the North Sea, the fort is no longer regularly manned. However, it was restored by the Harwich Society as a voluntary project in 1969. In summer, battle re-enactments and other events are held here. Part of the fort is now used as a museum. Just be careful circumnavigating the back in the summer on account of the thousands of bees!

Address Main Road, Harwich, CO12 3LT | **Getting there** The fort is 200 yards east of the A120 and 200 yards south of Harwich Town railway station | **Hours** Every Sun 10am–4pm, 1 May–30 Sept Thu–Sun 10am–4pm, Open Day Aug Bank Holiday | **Tip** Head 300 yards south to the Beacon Hill Battery fort on Barrack Lane, built during the reign of Henry VIII following his visit to the town in 1543 and now a scheduled ancient monument.

47 __ Mayflower Captain's House

Pilgrims, strangers sailing from a wearisome land

Christopher Jones was an everyday Harwich mariner of the 1590s who lived in this tiny cottage. He married a neighbour, the 17-year-old Sara Twitt, who lived opposite in what is now a pub, at Harwich's St Nicholas Church in December 1593. But it was his activities a few years later that made him a figure of international renown. He became Master of the *Mayflower*, the ship that made the perilous journey with the pilgrims across the Atlantic in 1620 to found one of the most famous American colonies.

Harwich could not have been much of a fun town then. It was run by hardline mariners and shipwrights who hanged witches in 1605 and dragged others through the streets for being harlots. Jones himself was up in front of the beak for keeping hunting dogs, a crime as he was not a gentleman.

No one knows where the *Mayflower* was built, but it was moored in Harwich. The port was the perfect place at the confluence of the Rivers Stour and Orwell with a safe natural harbour that had been used by warships for centuries. Indeed, during the Spanish Armada in 1588, Harwich amassed 17,000 troops to defend the country.

The year 2020 marked the 400th anniversary of the *Mayflower*'s pioneering voyage when it carried 102 passengers and 30 crew. Of all such expeditions, the *Mayflower*'s crossing has become the most legendary. On board were no ordinary passengers but the Pilgrim Fathers – religious dissidents, Puritans, in conflict with the Church of England, making a journey into the unknown to create a Garden of Eden in the New World. As one of the migrants noted about the England of the time: 'Cruelty and bloode is in our streetes, the land abowndeth with murthers, slaughters, incest, adulterers, whoredom, drunkeness, oppression and pride.' So nothing much changes.

Address 21 King's Head Street, Harwich, CO12 3EE | **Getting there** The captain's house is 50 yards south-east of the sea and 50 yards south of the Ha'penny Pier; train to Harwich Town | **Hours** Contact The Harwich Society www.harwich-society.co.uk/contact or +44 (0)1255 502872 for details of visits and guided tours during the summer | **Tip** Head to the Ha'penny Pier, a rare wooden promontory, to soak up the superb sea views and the chance to catch sight of a container ship the size of the Empire State Building gliding by.

48__ The Curiosity Cabinet

Readers of a squeamish disposition look away now

Cranfield's Curiosity Cabinet contains a most *outré* and outrageous amalgam of offerings, a crazy collection of curios, a carnival of crude delights. Here you can find taxidermy cryptids, obscure movie props, and displays of animal genitalia and medical specimens.

The shop is lit by lamps made from human and animal bone. The cabinet is a front room filled with stuffed beasts (filled with polyester, not Paxo) in a host of poses.

Folk with an appetite for the ridiculous can take home a stuffed three-headed duckling at £65 or a full mount zebra for £6,000. Some customers bring in things to add to the collection. One arrived with a frozen dead dog in a carrier bag.

A curtain entices you into a room with re-creations of famous screen monsters such as Gremlins or Klingons, and further on to Geoffrey, the eight-foot taxidermy giraffe and a selection of animal genitals that include North American bison scrotum sacks, kangaroo testicle bottle openers and a 22-inch walrus penis bone. There is a seasonally changing window display that might feature a human skeleton enjoying a can of beer from its deckchair, to Santa on the back of a swan swinging from the ceiling.

The shop is the brainchild of James Cranfield, who opened it in sedate Leigh in November 2013 after managing a jewellery store. When he was 10, his mother bought him a taxidermy red squirrel for Christmas and for his 13th birthday he was given a medical student grade skeleton, which he named Stanley. James has told journalists: 'I'm a bit desensitised to it all now. I will never get bored of it, I am a passionate collector. I'll be buying things until the day I die.'

Cranfield's Curiosity Cabinet has also become a popular place for dinner parties thrown by the rich and famous, as well as less tabloidish kids' birthday parties, a hoot if they don't succumb to the horrors of the horrible natural histories

Address 1193 London Road, Leigh-on-Sea, SS9 3JB, +44 (0)7763 051040, www.facebook.com/people/Cranfields-Curiosity-Cabinet | **Getting there** The shop is on the A13, the main road in the area, between Blenheim Crescent and Madeira Avenue; train to Leigh-on-Sea, then a short walk | **Hours** Mr. Cranfield posts his irregular opening hours on his social media channels (@thetaxidermist on Instagram and 'Cranfield's Curiosity Cabinet' on Facebook). Or by appointment, no purchase necessary. | **Tip** Head to the Broadway, Broadway West and Leigh Road in Leigh-on-Sea for funky, retro, quirky independent stores.

49_ Lee Brilleaux Bench
You got me on milk and alcohol

How do you like your rock 'n' roll served up? Baroque, stately, intellectual, awe-inspiring, like Southend's Procol Harum, or raw, rough, raucous and ready like Canvey's Dr Feelgood?

The Southend area doesn't get enough plaudits for its music heritage, but it has spawned those two major bands. Procol Harum came about in 1966 fronted by the multi-instrumentalist Gary Brooker who died in 2022. Brooker could not only play piano, organ, trombone, cornet and Bengal flute, but sing with a soulful determination influenced by Ray Charles. The group's name came from a mishearing of a friend's cat, Procul Harun, and in 1967 they created one of the best-known singles of all time, 'A Whiter Shade of Pale', one of only a few to sell more than 10 million copies but which hamstrung them for ever.

Interestingly, its follow-up, 'Homburg', in the same vein, was far more impressive. In their wake came two of the most magical albums in rock history: *Shine on Brightly* (1968) and *A Salty Dog* (1969), the haunting anthemic title track of the latter the most powerful nautical song ever written.

Ironically, the strongest reaction against the complexity of prog rock personified by Procol Harum also came from here. Dr Feelgood roared back to rock 'n' roll's primitive, primaeval origins in the mid-1970s. They were renowned for their manic live show heralded by the twin attack of brutal guitarist Wilko Johnson and raging vocalist Lee Brilleaux, who died of cancer aged only 42 in 1994. Lee Brilleaux's public image was simple but effective. He always looked like he'd just run a marathon in the Himalayas, and at the start of each tour would buy a gorgeous white suit jacket, which he would wear every night throughout the tour as it gathered beer and burger stains, sweat, toil, blood and tears, becoming the most famous jacket in rock.

This sedate commemorative bench barely does him justice.

Address Cliff Parade, Leigh-on-Sea, SS 9 1AS | Getting there Train to Chalkwell, then a short walk; by car, head east from Old Leigh village along the sea front | Hours Accessible 24 hours | Tip Head east to the centre of Southend, by the sea front, to see the latest fate befalling the sadly run-down Kursaal, once the centre of the local music scene, which opened in 1901 as the world's first purpose-built amusement park.

50__Old Leigh Fish Stalls
What's your poisson?

You've walked the thousand miles from Shoeburyness Danger Zone along the sea front, past the gaily-painted beach huts, the children's pleasure gardens, the world's longest pier, the obelisk marking the beginning of the Port of London's authority over the waters, and now after hours and hours of trekking you come across a most satisfying run of seafood stalls right by the water, offering fresh fare fished from the frothy foam.

The stalls and cockle sheds are located between Old Leigh village and Leigh-on-Sea station. Can there be anywhere in England more perfect for selling cockles, mussels, prawns and jellied eels? Typical is Osborne's, a family-run business with a stall in the centre of the retail row and a café in the centre of Old Leigh village. The café is based in an 18th-century stable mews clad in weatherboard timber, whose horses delivered ale to pubs such as the local Crooked Billet across the road.

Fishing locally dates back far. Leigh's sheltered position allowed it to grow into a large and prosperous port, renowned for its cockles, which were raked from the seabed by hand between tides all year round. Cocklers would carry a yoke laden with two baskets from the boat to where the cockles were steam cooked and then separated from the shells by sieving. Before 1820, the catch was transported to London by boat up the Thames, the fish kept in pits in Leigh until the journey could be made. A regular night service by road was then started until the railways took over.

The second most popular pastime was smuggling. When the Peterboat Inn here caught fire in 1892, a search under the cellar revealed a trove of illegal contraband. Over the years, several tunnels have been discovered. These would have been used not just for storing smuggled stuff but by young men trying to avoid the press gangs that strode the streets looking for dupes to man the yardarm.

Address Cockle Sheds, High Street, Leigh-on-Sea, SS 9 2ER | **Getting there** Train to Leigh-on Sea; by car, head west from Old Leigh village along the sea front or east from Leigh-on-Sea station – park at the station | **Hours** Normal retail hours | **Tip** Take time to explore magical Old Leigh village where the wind whistles through the rigging and a salty smack on the lips suggests a serving of seafood salad soon.

51__ Two Tree Island

First there is a tree then another, yes there is

One of the most forgotten tiny islands by the Thames lies just north-east of Canvey. Two Tree Island covers just 640 acres and is connected to the mainland at Leigh-on-Sea by a single span bridge. The island, for long known as Leigh Marsh, was reclaimed from the estuary in the 18th century when a seawall was built around the saltmarsh, and it was used as pasture land until 1910 when a sewage works was built.

A worse fate befell the site in 1936 when the entire island began to be used for landfill. It was later saved, capped and reseeded with grass, and converted into a nature reserve. The saltmarsh fields have plentiful golden samphire, sea purslane, common sea-lavender and sea aster. Here you can escape urban blight and suburban ennui by immersing yourself in an environment where it feels like land is slipping irrevocably into the sea. During winter, the mudflats offer the perfect habitat for thousands of wildfowl and waders, and noisy flocks of dark-bellied Brent geese that love the dense beds of eel-grass. In the lagoon on the west side, avocets feed, and gulls and great tits nest, patrolled by voles and stoats, although a nest watch had to be organised to prevent the stealing of avocet eggs. To aid humans, a concrete jetty is operated by the Port of London Authority. There are four miles of trails, scouts utilise the water, and model aircraft lovers have a site for air shows.

But there are also reminders of the grim times of two world wars, with pillboxes right by the water on the east side. These were used for communication and signals, and to repel invaders. The firing loops that allowed Bren light machine guns to pivot can be seen, but the pillboxes are becoming a victim to severe weathering, and the roofs have almost caved in. It's not just war that can be a problem. During the North Sea Floods of 1953 two sewage workers had to be rescued by boat from a shed roof on the island.

Address Belton Way, Leigh-on-Sea, SS 9 2GB | Getting there Head south from Leigh-on-Sea station towards the sea – there aren't many choices in getting there | Hours Accessible 24 hours | Tip For more nature, head two miles north-west to explore Hadleigh Country Park with its superb views of the estuary.

52 The Bible Murals Church
'Overlay the walls with gold and graved cherubims'

From the outside it looks plain, but inside St Nicholas is a phantasmagorical wonder. That's because the Rev Ernest Geldart, rector 1881–1900, highly decorated the church with remarkable and copious stencils, murals and representations.

St Nicholas was built about 1120 with a wooden belfry and two bells. When Father Ernest took over, he carved a piscina, refurbished the seating, and installed new stained glass. In 1886 he turned to aesthetics, covering virtually every surface with a variety of idiosyncratic pictures, texts and symbolic designs, citing that 'God's house ought to be the finest and most beautiful house in the parish'. The scenes include a painting of Bethlehem with Christ, Mary, Joseph and the shepherds, a picture of Saint John the Baptist preaching, and a painting depicting the Creed. There are also symbols, patterns, Latin inscriptions and a stained-glass window of St Nicholas.

And did the people bow humbly? Nay. There were considerable complaints, not just for the *outré* designs, but because the work coincided with liturgical changes involving candles, incense and processions – 'the work of the Pope,' Protestant detractors cried. Detractors flooded the papers with letters and even threatened to prosecute before calming down. The décor is much more appreciated today. The walls were cleaned and restored in 1992 and the colours still amaze. Church warden Pam Booker says the paintings and decoration give the church a great atmosphere. 'It feels like a home almost. Doing a service when the candles are lit, it has a lovely spiritual feel about it that we all appreciate.' Indeed, the midnight service sees the church lit by a hundred candles.

The parish, on the east side of the River Blackwater, unites Little Braxted with Wickham Bishops and is one of the smallest in the country. Indeed, the church itself only seats about 60 and rarely gets a *minyan*.

Address Little Braxted Lane, Little Braxted, CM8 3EU, +44 (0)1621 892867 | **Getting there** This little gem of a church is tucked away in a beautiful setting and could easily be missed, but it is only half a mile from Junction 22 on the A12 | **Hours** Viewable from the outside 24 hours and inside during services | **Tip** Head to the Green Man pub in Little Braxted. Very apt, given that the Green Man is an ancient pagan symbol of fertility found on many church walls.

53__ The PitStop
Oi! Who do you think you are, Stirling Moss?

Calling all budding Lewis Hamiltons and Michael Schumachers. Slow down, double de-clutch and park up for a most unusual pit stop at the PitStop. It's the Rutter family's unique motor racing-themed hotel and diner just off the M11 near Hatfield Forest.

Melvyn Rutter has a thing about Morgan sports cars. This was the company founded in 1910 by Henry Morgan who made his name two years later coming second in the Light Car & Cyclecar speed competition at Brooklands, Surrey, the country's main race track, and whose cars were famously made of wood. He and his wife, who drives a Pink Lady, chose to honour the fast brand here in 2009. Each room has an individual flavour. The Drop Head Coupé room is named after the exotic sports car that featured a folding roof and a sloping rear. Within is a taste of the Indian Raj. The drapes come from the sub-continent, the bathroom is golden, and it has underfloor heating. The Aero room is dedicated to the Morgan Aero 8 sports car, the company's first supercar. Oak is the main feature, and there is a solar-powered blackout blind and colour-changing lighting in the mosaic bathroom.

Need refuelling after all that vicarious motor racing? Try the in-house diner, blasted in heavy red with a spectacular mix of old Americana, *circa* 1957, in best *Back to the Future* style, merged with memories of the legendary Ace Cafe on the North Circular Road. Its furnishings were salvaged from the original 1905-built Morgan factory and include steel lampshades, bar stools imported from across the pond, and an obligatory vintage 1960s pinball machine. The American-styled fridge can be accessed 24/7.

For a final treat, anyone with one of those new-fangled road-access approval sheets – a driving licence in plain English – can hire one of the Morgan cars. Just don't get too carried away and start spraying champagne over everyone when returning to base.

Address The PitStop, The Morgan Garage, Little Hallingbury, CM22 7RA, +44 (0)1279 725725 & +44 (0)7803 290000 after 6pm, www.thepitstop.net | Getting there The garage is on the A1060, three miles north-east of Sawbridgeworth; train to Sawbridgeworth and a taxi ride or 30-minute walk | Hours Open normal garage and hotel hours | Tip Need even more automobilian exhilaration? Head to Stansted Raceway, 10 minutes' drive from Stansted Airport, to watch action-packed stockcar, banger and hotrod racing.

54 Zeppelin Village
What was and should never have been

It wasn't just during World War II that the enemy attacked by air. One of the few airborne attacks on Essex in the Great War occurred on the night of 23 and 24 September, 1916 when two enormous German Zeppelin airships crashed in the county. One came down in a ball of flames in Great Burstead, killing all 22 crew. The other, L 33, having dropped bombs on the East End of London killing six people, wrecking a pub, and setting an oil depot on fire, was heading back to Germany when it was hit by an anti-aircraft shell and crash landed here in Little Wigborough.

The airship's 650-foot-long body buckled as it landed, and occupants of the nearest house were lucky to escape with their lives. The German commander, Kapitanleutnant Alois Böcker, set fire to the wreckage and then paradoxically tried to warn locals in the vicinity who unsurprisingly refused to open their doors. All the canvas was burnt off, just leaving the aluminium frame. A white terrier dog hounding around at the time was scorched brown by the heat.

Böcker and his crew then headed down the road and bumped into policeman Charles Smith, later for ever known as Zepp Smith. He was shocked at being asked directions by soldiers with German accents. When one officer asked him in English what he thought about the war, PC Smith decided it was time for his 'for you, Fritz, the war is over' impersonation and arrested him.

The jolly Germans turned out to be the only armed enemy soldiers to land in Britain during the Great War. They were taken to Mersea Island, where they were looked after by the vicar in the parish hall, and then handed over to the military. Just to add to the farce, a baby girl born locally that night was named Zeppelina. The fashion for naming nippers after aircraft never took off, but the eventual Zepp Williams lived to a ripe old age and has a memorial in Little Wigborough Church.

Address Copt Hall Lane, Little Wigborough, CO5 7RD | Getting there Little Wigborough is 8 miles south of Colchester on the way to the Blackwater National Nature Reserve | Hours Accessible 24 hours | Tip Forget the horrors of war and head south to Copt Hall Marshes to breathe in the fresh sea air and savour the wide-open skies. Lots of birds, wildflowers and untainted dogs.

55 Simon Beck's Slag Heap

Après ski, le déluge

To some people it's a banal, nothing-much piece of land made up of the spoil moved from St Pancras when they built the British Library in the 1990s. But to the perspicacious psychogeographer, it's a striking slice of urban detritus with a suitably strange and sinister history. In 1870, the Gas, Light and Coke Company arrived with big ideas. They built houses, dug garden allotments and provided all the trimmings on a 400-acre site named Beckton after the guv'nor, Simon Adams Beck.

At its peak, Beckton Gas Works supplied the formidable fuel to four million Londoners as well as manufacturing by-products such as fertilisers, inks and dyes. During World War II, there was the obligatory on-site prisoner of war camp. The works closed in 1976. In its place came Beckton Alp, a Swiss-styled ski slope on top of toxic spoil, the air somewhat less cool, less canton-fresh and more A13 petrol-fumed than you normally find where people throw themselves off mountain sides. You really could dry ski there, as Princess Diana discovered in 1989.

Even this stopped in 2001. Plans to create SnowWorld, an indoor ski slope, foundered when potential developers realised they couldn't overcome the massive contamination. Instead, the site is now a nature reserve, which must be really trying for the assorted flora and fauna. Nearby is the eastern terminus of the Northern Outfall Sewer which, one hopes, no longer pours raw waste into the nearby Thames thanks to the building of a sewage works, the largest in the country, treating over 200 million gallons a day. There are scintillating views back towards Docklands in what is one of the most charmless areas of the country.

Such is the *outré*, post-apocalyptic nature of the locale, film companies have queued up to hire the space, most famously Stanley Kubrick for the last hour of his 1987 Vietnam film *Full Metal Jacket*.

Address Beckton, E 6 | Getting there The site is just west of the A 1020 as it heads by the roundabout | Hours Accessible 24 hours | Tip The area is more water than land. What is now Gallions Point Marina was for decades Royal Albert Dock from the days when London was one of the world's greatest ports, but closed in 1981. On the south side is the airport no one knows about: the incongruously named London City.

56 Biggest UK Council Estate
Ennui east of the East End

The unstoppable expansion of London into the 20th century resulted in Becontree, and it soon became not just the country's but the world's biggest council estate. Becontree came about through cynical government belief that the best way to prevent the war-weary from succumbing to the new revolutionary trappings of Bolshevism was, in the words of Juvenal the second century Roman poet, to give them 'bread and circuses', that municipal socialism was preferable to revolutionary communism.

Becontree went up from 1919. The poor were decamped from the teeming slums of the East End further east into the countryside. Except, once it was finished, it was no longer countryside. Instead, it was mass housing – low-rise cottagey, *rus in urbe*-styled simple, solid properties. The displaced now had things hitherto unseen: a front garden, a back garden, a bath, an inside toilet and lots of greenery all around. What they no longer had though were the other fripperies that make life so exciting: their old community, its pubs, sweet shops, sweat shops, workplaces, caffs and familiar streets.

All the latest fashions in town planning went into Becontree, based around the utopian ideals published by Ebenezer Howard in books such as *Garden Cities*, 1902. A zonal system meant that the estate had no industry – the dirty worky stuff was well away from the houses. That looked great in the town hall committee rooms, and was definitely a boon for the inhabitants' breathing, but it also meant that they had to travel far to earn a crust. Worse still, there was little commercial development. Shops of a sort would come later. In the meantime, were people meant to grow their own?

Becontree was finished in 1935, by which time it had a population of around 100,000 in 26,000 homes. Its main problem was that it was boring – tediously life-sappingly boring. Like a benign open prison, and still is.

Address The first houses, honoured by a plaque, are at 22–28 Chittys Lane, Becontree, RM8 1UP | **Getting there** The vast never-ending estate is between Chadwell Heath railway station to the north and Becontree tube station to the south. Chadwell Heath station is 400 yards north of Chittys Lane. | **Hours** Accessible 24 hours | **Tip** For something more historic, head west to busy boorish Barking and the ruins of Barking Abbey, once one of the most important monasteries in the country.

57 _ Ford's

'Any color so long as it is black'

One of the most famous names in motor car history opened this plant by the Thames in 1931, and it eventually became the biggest of its kind in Europe. When Henry Ford first came to Britain he went to Manchester – to Trafford Park – where the docks had quick access west to America and there he produced the famed Model T. After a few years he realised he needed to be on the eastern, European, side of Britain where there were deeper water docks. So, over one weekend in September 1931, specially chartered trains brought 1,500 workers south.

Production started the following day, and the first Ford AA truck rolled off the line on 1 October, 1931. For the workers, Ford's was not much fun. One unnamed employee recalled how 'at Ford the worker was a robot, part of the ever-flowing mechanism. The work was exceedingly monotonous; everything organised to suppress the individual personality'. Ford employees were obliged to wear a one-piece uniform and badge, and those who turned up at the gate without them would be sent home, their pay docked for the time taken before they returned. Nor was trade union membership allowed. However, wages were high and jobs were at a premium. Even the floor sweepers were paid as much as five pounds a week, which between the wars put them in the working-class aristocracy.

The plant produced some of the best-loved cars in British history: the Zephyr, Zodiac, Cortina, as well as some that should have stayed locked-up in the garage, like the Anglia. In the end more than 11 million cars, trucks and tractors were made here at London's largest manufacturing site. Placed end to end they would stretch more than 10 times around the world. Vehicle assembly stopped in 2002 with the Ford Fiesta, and production moved to Spain. Today, the latest advanced technology is deployed for making engines, turbines and dealing with logistics.

Address Ripple Road, Dagenham, RM9 6SA | **Getting there** By car, take the unlovely A13 to the junction with the A1306 – Dagenham Dock station is just south of the plant | **Hours** Viewable from the outside only | **Tip** Unexpectedly, Ford's Dagenham estate is home to a rich variety of wildlife around the Breach, a natural lake, formed when the River Thames burst its banks more than 300 years ago. New drivers on site are warned to be aware of wildlife crossing the roads.

58 Itchycoo Park
It's all too beautiful

It's one of the most famous pieces of music in the universe. The Small Faces' glorious sparkling summertime 1967 psychedelic romp with words that cheer every wayward child: 'You can miss out school (won't that be cool)/Why go to learn the words of fools?' And there's the triumphant chorus: 'It's all too beauty–fuu–uul.'

But where is the actual Itchycoo Park? Steve Marriott, whose soulful strains powered the famed mod band, cited unlovable Little Ilford Park in Manor Park by the roaring North Circular A 406 and the smelly River Roding. But bass player Ronnie Lane, who wrote most of the song, put the location here in Valentine's Park, a gorgeous stretch of tranquil greenery in an unlovable part of London Essex left over from Epping Forest. While writing the song, Ronnie Lane was poring over pictures of Oxford, hence the opening line: 'Over Bridge of Sighs.' The 'itchy' came from the stinging nettles that flourished in the park. Schoolchildren would drop the seeds of rose hips down a dupe's collar. More itching. There was also the added danger of being stung by the plentiful wasps.

'Itchycoo Park' was recorded at Britain's, or possibly the world's, greatest recording studio – Olympic in Barnes on the other side of London. The much-loved single was one of the first ever records to feature flanging: an electronic effect characterised by an easily identifiable sweeping sound. It also uses unsynchronised tape recordings to add to the soup of sublimely swooshing sounds. The BBC initially wanted the song banned for alleged drug references. 'What did you do there? We got high-igh.' A few quiet words from the management and the Beeb caved in.

Sadly, both those band members met tragic ends. Ronnie Lane contracted multiple sclerosis after recording a superb slice of folk with 'The Poacher' (1974) and the unimpeachable Marriott perished in a house fire in 1991.

Address Cranbrook Road, Ilford, IG1 4TG | **Getting there** The park is just south-east of the junction of the A12 Eastern Avenue and Cranbrook Road; Underground to Gants Hill (Central Line) | **Hours** Open daily from 8am, but closing hours vary with the seasons – check visionrcl.org.uk to avoid getting locked in at night | **Tip** Inside the park is Valentine's Mansion, a stately home built 1696 for Lady Tillotson, the widow of the late Archbishop of Canterbury. Visitors can explore the many period rooms and visit the gallery, which has year-round exhibitions.

59 Tube Tunnel Plane Factory

Airtight manufactory

World War II is on. Planes have to be built amidst the utmost secrecy, so where better to make them than inside a tube tunnel? Why under Gants Hill? The tube here, the eastern extension to the Central Line, taking trains from the City of London into deepest Essex, had been built but was still not ready for use. Perfect.

The 300,000-square-foot subterranean factory was completed in March 1942 at a cost of £500,000, and operated by the electronics company Plessey who persuaded the Air Ministry and London Transport to let them use the unfinished tunnel connecting Leytonstone and Gants Hill after their factory in nearby Ilford was bombed. Here, under the arterial Eastern Avenue, now one of the nastiest roads in the region, the mostly young female workforce of 4,000 made wiring sets for Halifax and Lancaster bombers, wireless equipment, field telephones, and electro mechanical devices used by cryptologists such as Alan Turing at Bletchley Park.

There was extra special protection from bombs using soil spilled from the construction of the deep level shelters in central London to build up depth. But there was also the added danger of the nearby River Roding, and so watertight doors were installed. Working conditions were not auspicious. Staff began at 7.30am and they couldn't even get the tube here; the mini-railway simply carried components along. Overtime was unpaid and there was no smoking. Not many people labour with only artificial light and limited air, but at least the workers could come up above ground to go to the loo.

The station opened in 1947. Now the public could marvel at Charles Holden's stunning design influenced by the Moscow subway. Today, if you know where to look, there is a brick structure stuck between two nearby houses on Eastern Avenue that disguises a ventilation shaft built to carry goods in and out of the factory.

Address Cranbrook Road, Gants Hill, IG2 6UD | Getting there Underground to Gants Hill (Central Line); by car, along the Eastern Avenue (A 12) to the mega junction with Cranbrook Road and Woodford Avenue | Hours Normal tube hours | Tip Head out of the station and along Woodford Avenue to the nearby Shalom Hot Beigel Bakery, world-renowned centre for authentic Jewish food.

60 __ The IRA Man's Church

'We Ourselves'

The strangely named church of the Holy Trinity and St Augustine of Hippo in Leytonstone would be of no interest but for one unassuming event. In February 1928 the infant John Stephenson was baptised here as a Protestant.

Who? Stephenson had a most unusual life for someone born in so mundane a setting. He was chief of staff for the IRA from 1969–72. Not bad for an Englishman who spoke with an estuary accent and didn't share the religious background of his colleagues. How did this remarkable progression pan out? At the age of seven, Stephenson's mother told him: 'I'm Irish, therefore you're Irish… Don't forget it.' As he grew up, he became increasingly involved with Irish organisations and joined Sinn Féin, the political wing of the IRA. Rising through the ranks of this formidable organisation – terrorists to most in England, but not to most in Ireland – he changed his name with a deft sleight of hand to the Gaelic version, Seán Mac Stíofáin.

In July 1953, Mac Stíofáin took part in a daring IRA raid, liberating arms from the Officers' Training Corps base at Felsted School in Dunmow, Essex. The usurpers seized more than 100 rifles and mortar bombs, and made off in a van, but were stopped by the police; the vehicle was so overloaded it was going at only 20 mph and traffic was queuing behind. Mac Stíofáin got eight years.

Twenty years later, Mac Stíofáin was caught up in something even more remarkable. In July 1972, the bloodiest year of the Troubles, he led the IRA delegation to the most controversial secret government meeting of the era. At a Tory MP's house in Chelsea (recently bought by Roman Abramovich for £26.6 million) the Northern Ireland Secretary, Willie Whitelaw, debated not just with Mac Stíofáin but with Martin McGuinness and Gerry Adams, whisked out of jail in Ireland for the talks, just for the day. Would you believe there is no tribute in the church?

Address 4 Holloway Road, Leytonstone, E 11 4LD | Getting there The church is just north of Langthorne Park and west of the B 161 (High Road, Leytonstone); Leyton tube station is half a mile west | Hours Viewable from the outside 24 hours and inside during services (www.e11holy.org.uk) | Tip Just to the west is St Patrick's Catholic Cemetery where it is quite difficult to find the grave of Mary Kelly, fifth and possible final victim of Jack the Ripper. This could be because she is said to have been spotted very much alive after her 'murder'.

LONDON ESSEX, LEYTONSTONE

61 No Motorway Protest Road

Just a slip of a road

In the early 1990s, Claremont Road became the focus of a bitter battle over the building of a roaring, raucous and completely unnecessary dual carriageway, the A12 extension, aka the four-mile M11 Link Road. The route had first been proposed in the 1960s at a time when pen-twitching council highways officers across London were planning to ruin the capital by criss-crossing it with flyovers, motorways and ring roads, having watched too many episodes of *Thunderbirds*. When they failed to wreck Hampstead Heath, they turned their attention to softer targets such as humdrum, forgettable, dreary suburban Leytonstone, where the residents were not as organised in their opposition. Protestors noted sarcastically that the way things were going, the whole of residential London would soon be replaced with dual carriageways. By the 1990s, the planned road was cited as a vital link between the M11 motorway and the newly revived Docklands.

Initially, protest centred on George Green in Wanstead, a mile away, where a 250-year-old sweet chestnut tree earmarked for destruction was occupied by the 'Dongas' – direct action environmental campaigners using the very latest technology, mobile phones, to out-manoeuvre the police. When the tree was axed nonetheless, protesters squatted some of the 350 houses that had been acquired here by compulsory purchase, most notably on Claremont Road. Many residents were determined to resist eviction. Ninety-two-year-old Dolly Watson refused to leave her home, supporting the protestors by declaring that 'They're not dirty hippy squatters, they're the grandchildren I never had'.

Nevertheless, the road was built, opening in 1999, and Claremont Road truncated. It wasn't long before it was clear that the link road had increased congestion rather than solving it, as well as wrecking what had been a quiet community minding its own business.

Address Claremont Road, Leytonstone, E 11 4EE | **Getting there** Don't take the A 12 as there is no access to Claremont Road – better to keep to the local roads; Leytonstone tube station is a mile north-east | **Hours** Viewable from the outside 24 hours | **Tip** Solve one of the most difficult local mysteries by exploring Leytonstone, looking for traces of the area's greatest native – Alfred Hitchcock. See if you can find the murals, mosaics, a pub and a hotel.

62 The Station to Nowhere

A bit of Essex in Kent, or the other way round?

A gorgeous Italianate building (often covered with scaffolding), the biggest in the locale, is the dead terminus of the most abused railway in London, which translates as 'Welcome to the closed down North Woolwich station on the North London Railway'.

Originally, the Eastern Counties and Thames Junction company opened a line here in the 1840s so that workers on the Essex side of the big river could get to their vital jobs at the Royal Arsenal in Woolwich proper on the south side. As the trains could not float, they disembarked, as the railway authorities like to say (in English, got off the train) at North Woolwich station and transferred to a ferry. A few years later the land to the west was transformed into huge and successful docks accompanied by warehouses, factories, workers' houses and pubs.

What had been marshland did not thrive. The docks withered away as a workplace, and the railway line from North Woolwich back into civilisation was constantly rejigged, shut down, reopened, renamed and run down. Yet some rewarding investment has appeared. In 1984, BT opened the excitingly named London North Woolwich Earth Station locally at Pier Road. It was London's first satellite earth station conveying information on financial services for bankers in the City of London.

Yes, yes, yes, but the well-travelled *flâneur* will interject to say 'Isn't Woolwich on the south bank of the Thames and therefore tradition-ally in Kent?'. Exactly. How did a tiny, obscure, unlovable tract of land on the north bank of the Thames, which should be in Essex, get the Woolwich name? It's all the fault of Hamo, steward to William the Conqueror, who was given manors on both side of the Thames. Some believe that what is now North Woolwich could have been the original Woolwich, later lending its name to what became the larger settlement across the river.

Address Pier Road, North Woolwich, E 16 2FH | **Getting there** Obviously not by train any more!, so take the A 112, south of London City Airport on this narrow sliver of land | **Hours** Accessible 24 hours | **Tip** The ferries still run as a vital free service. Just don't get the one named Ernest Bevin, for it is named after the ruthless 1940s Labour foreign secretary who promoted Britain's first atomic bombs.

63 The Thames Barrier
Before the Flood

Remember those climate change disaster films, *The Day After Tomorrow*, or the lesser-known but equally worrying *Killer Flood: The Day the Dam Broke*? Well, here's the epic installation that keeps London safe from Armageddon – the Thames Barrier.

The Thames Barrier, a wonder of engineering, was built to prevent the capital disappearing under the water. Work began in 1974, the official opening by Queen Elizabeth took place in 1984, and it cost more than £450 million. The barrier has 10 steel gates that reach 1,700 feet across the water, and are raised monthly for testing. When open, the gates lie flat on the river floor. They close by being rotated upwards to block the river. The idea behind its design of retractable gates came from Charles Draper who was inspired at his parents' house in Wood Green by the shape of the taps on a gas cooker.

The Thames is tidal right through the heart of London, all the way out west to Teddington Lock. The threat of flooding comes from the North Sea with its high spring tides and sudden surges, often caused by a depression in north Scotland. The barrier has been well used. It has witnessed more than 200 flood defence closures. Meanwhile, there have been 15 boat collisions, fortunately without serious damage. The barrier is a well-used feature for dramas. In one grim episode of *Spooks*, terrorists threaten to blow it up to swamp London and kill the millions unable to escape quickly enough. In real life, when staff threatened to strike in 2019, the *Sun* newspaper warned that 30-foot waves might engulf London. Now the authorities are thinking of more barriers, maybe in Tilbury or right out at sea in Southend.

Instead of just gazing in awe at this ingenious creation, visit the Information Centre that explains its sinister purpose. The Centre offers regular tours, an occasional highlight being a trip underneath.

Address South of North Woolwich Road, E 16 2GP | Getting there DLR to Pontoon Dock | Hours Accessible to see either from the river on a boat trip, or from Thames Barrier Park. Or contact the Information Centre on the south bank of the Thames to join a group tour (booking essential) | Tip Why not head *over* the Thames? A handily-placed cable car, a mile or so west, offers superb watery views.

64 __ Boleyn Tavern
Not Anne Boleyn's local

A most magnificent and grandiose late Victorian drinking emporium with a baroque corner tower, and historic football and royal connections, stands proudly just yards from the site of the much-lamented Boleyn ground, better known as Upton Park, long-time home of perennially unsuccessful football club West Ham United who pointlessly moved a few miles north-west to the Olympic Stadium in 2016.

The Boleyn Tavern is named after an older and also vanished local structure, Boleyn Castle, a 16th-century turreted property where, according to an Uncle Albert-ish legend, Henry VIII began courting Anne Boleyn, the wife he later had beheaded, in 1536. The grounds were rented to West Ham when the club moved to the site in 1904, but Boleyn Castle was damaged in the Blitz and demolished in 1955.

The pub naturally became a favourite with the football fraternity, who would down copious pints of undrinkable lager within, before and after matches, indeed sometimes during, having forgotten why they had come here in the first place. Opposing fans, especially Millwall, Arsenal or Chelsea, were not welcome. But on non-match days all was still and calm. One day in 1931 none other than Mahatma Gandhi came in for an uplifting glass of water, the great spiritual leader being opposed to alcohol and even tea, which he gave up and later insulted.

Now, with the football gone, the pub has been gloriously restored. It is listed on CAMRA's inventory of pubs with outstanding historic interiors. There's a huge horseshoe-shaped bar, Britain's longest, and marble floors of Carrara stone from Italian quarries. An Art Nouveau coloured-glass skylight spans the former billiards room. The walls are lined with match programmes and pictures of legendary players such as Bobby Moore and Geoff Hurst. Just don't start singing 'I'm Forever Blowing Bubbles' in your excitement at finding the pub.

Address 1 Barking Road, East Ham, E6 1PW, +44 (0)208 472 2182, www.boleyntavern.co.uk | Getting there The pub is by the junction of the A124 and the B167; Underground to Upton Park (District Line) | Hours Mon–Wed 4–11pm, Thu noon–11pm, Fri & Sat noon–1am, Sun noon–10pm | Tip Head up Green Street, which runs north-south, for a cornucopia of Asian wares and curries.

65 The Doctor Who Shop
It's like the Tardis in there

From the street it looks like just another shop, but when you get inside time travels in all directions, space expands, and strange aliens, Daleks and cyborgs rush to assist the unwary customer. If only. It's really the Dr Who shop and museum. Here you can buy everything you might need for a journey through time and space. Fancy a Tardis Makeup Bag or a King Size Tardis Duvet Bedding Set? Maybe an 11th Doctor Sonic Screwdriver Pizza Cutter – in case they've run short on Planet 4-X-Alpha-4, or a Tardis Projection Alarm Clock. Most important of all, a 500-year diary.

Doctor Who was first broadcast by the BBC in 1963 and became immediately identifiable by its astonishing electro soundtrack composed by Delia Derbyshire, a major influence on Kraftwerk. The programme has become a world-wide cult classic as the longest-running sci-fi television show on the planet, and possibly on other planets, as well as the most successful sci-fi series of all time based on broadcast ratings, and DVD and book sales.

The first of 13 Time Lords was William Hartnell. The most celebrated was Tom Baker, with his flowing coloured scarf. The most unlikely, Jodie Whittaker, the first woman doctor, in 2017. As each doctor comes to the end of their stint they transform effortlessly and even transgenderly into a new incarnation.

As anyone who has ever owned a TV set knows, the Time Lord occupies an old-fashioned police box, which internally is a few thousand times bigger than how it looks from the outside. Nothing ever goes smoothly for the good doctors. While travelling through time to help people in need, they are accosted by various ne'er-do-wells, most appallingly the Daleks – violent, merciless aliens modelled on the Nazis, determined to conquer the universe and eliminate inferior races, all of whom, incongruously, can move faster than the Daleks. They haven't got to Upton Park yet.

Address The Who Shop, 39–41 Barking Road, Upton Park, E6 1PY, +44 (0)208 471 2356, www.thewhoshop.com | Getting there Underground to Upton Park (District Line), then a short walk | Hours Shop: Mon–Sat 9.30am–5.30pm; museum: Thu–Sat 11am–3pm | Tip You won't need the Tardis to find the excellent Newham Bookshop, very close by at 743–745 Barking Road.

66 World Champions

Fake Jules Rimet still gleaming

It's one of the most famous poses in English football history. Four World Cup winners – Bobby Moore, Geoff Hurst and Martin Peters, who all played locally for West Ham, plus Everton's Ray Wilson – with the top prize, the Jules Rimet Trophy, minutes after England won the World Cup in 1966.

Except it's not that simple. Although Bobby Moore did receive the actual real Jules Rimet trophy from the Queen after the final whistle in front of an incredulous country, the football authorities swapped it for a replica before the players went out onto the pitch… in case the real one got nicked. That wasn't paranoid. The real thing had been stolen from a Westminster building only a few months before the tournament and then magically found by a dog, Pickles, miles away.

We need Pickles back, for no one now knows where the real Jules Rimet Trophy is. For the next World Cup in Mexico in 1970 the English Football Association handed FIFA, the game's governing body, the replica. When Brazil won the tournament, which was for a record third time, they were allowed to keep the Jules Rimet Trophy for good, but were given the replica. It was later stolen, ironic given that when thieves took it in England, Brazil said that would never have happened in their country, where even robbers love football too much.

By then the real World Cup was hidden under the bed of the FA's silversmith, George Bird. Twice his house was burgled but thieves failed to find it. After Bird died in 1995 the Cup was auctioned by Sotheby's. Described as the real thing, it sold for £254,500. The successful buyer? FIFA. They then brought in experts to examine their expensive acquisition only to discover that they had indeed bought another replica – made of bronze!

Philip Jackson's statue stands a goal-kick from the site of West Ham United's former ground. Just to add to the fun, it was unveiled in 2003 by Prince Andrew.

Address Green Street, Upton Park, E 13 9ER | Getting there Underground to Upton Park (District Line) | Hours Accessible 24 hours | Tip Fans come from around the world – okay from somewhere else in London – to find any remaining sign of West Ham's famous stadium, especially the legendary Chicken Run, but are disappointed because the ground has been demolished.

67 __ The Ruined Village Green
Going back to its roots

It was a peaceful village green – George Green to be exact – identified by a gorgeous sweet chestnut tree 250 years old, a remnant of Epping Forest, which once covered the lands east of the River Lea boundary with London. Under its leaves many a courting couple smooched, and intellectuals sprawled to read Conrad or T. E. Lawrence.

Then, in the 20th century, London began to spread eastwards. They extended the tube and built a station opposite. In the 1990s, worse still: they announced that that environmental horror – the motorway – was going to be built underneath the village green. The tree would have to go, so the man said, roots, foundations everything, for the cut and cover tunnel along with a large number of houses that had become blighted, unsurprisingly, by the motorway plans.

Nevertheless protestors, possibly led by *Coronation Street*'s Spider Nugent, took root. Some began to live inside what was now The Tree. They even secured it a postcode, the only tree in the country so blessed (E 11 1AA, also that of the local post office). This was now a far more newsworthy campaign than letters to the papers and dull public meetings. The Tree received international attention. A lollipop lady, Jean Gosling, rallied support from children (and was later fired from her job for doing so while wearing her uniform). Fences went up and protestors tore them down. Early in the morning of 7 December, 1993, police evicted the protesters and The Tree came down.

Wanstead and beyond now has a pointless and unnecessary motorway, and George Green is ruined. Who wants to laze away a summer Sunday afternoon with the nation's traffic underneath? Protestors now look forward to an eco-friendly future when motorways are consigned to the dustbin of history and trees are grown back. Just need to find somebody with some preserved twigs, branches and leaves of old faithful to replant it.

Address The Green, Wanstead, E 11 2NT | Getting there Underground to Wanstead (Central Line) or A 12 Eastern Avenue. Don't use the motorway on principle! | Hours Accessible 24 hours | Tip To the south is the less-affected Wanstead Park, originally formal landscape around grand Wanstead House, now gone. In its place are grazing Longhorn cattle, most incongruous in suburban London.

68 Anti-Air War Memorial
Air war, what is it good for? Absolutely nothing

Sadly, this structure in Woodford Green is all that's left of the local presence of one of Britain's greatest ever political campaigners: Sylvia Pankhurst, daughter of the better-known suffragette Emmeline.

Sylvia Pankhurst was not just one of the leaders of the long-running and ultimately successful early 20th-century suffragette campaign to get women the vote, she was also a highly talented artist and an exciting writer. Yet she forsook her career to campaign vociferously. When women finally gained the vote on the same terms as men in 1928, she moved on to her next political project, opposition to Italy's colonisation of east Africa. No one was interested then in this Italian thing, fascism.

After World War II, Sylvia moved into a proto-hippie-cum-bohemian community here in Woodford Green on the fringes of Epping Forest. She eventually emigrated to the east Africa she had so nobly defended, and became a heroine of Ethiopia. This memorial, built on land she owned opposite the Red Cottage where she lived, since demolished, remembers her staunch pacifist beliefs that so annoyed MI5 during the Great War they dubbed her 'the tiresome Miss Pankhurst'. Sylvia herself commissioned this, Britain's first anti-air war memorial, in 1935, when war in the air was still a new phenomenon, but one that was to devastate both sides in the next war.

One of the inscriptions on the memorial dedicates it to *those who in 1932 upheld the right to use bombing aeroplanes*, a sarcastic reference to the participants of a conference that year who voted to maintain the right to use aerial bombing in warfare. Or, as the sculptor Eric Benfield, explained: 'Those who had preserved bombing were politically and morally dead, and this was their gravestone.' In 1996 the stone bomb at the top was stolen but later found in Epping Forest. Sylvia's son, Richard, and the local borough paid for the repairs.

Address Woodford Green, opposite Hills of Woodford Toyota, Woodford, IG8 0RD |
Getting there Woodford Green, the road, is the A104; Woodford tube station is a mile
south-east | Hours Accessible 24 hours | Tip A suffragette's stone's throw from the memorial
is Highbeam House 'luxury' homes, built on the site of Sylvia Pankhurst's Red Cottage, next
to what she called Suffragette Gardens, a centre for radical activity a hundred years ago.

69 Churchill Usually Defaced

We will wipe the graffiti. We will never surrender

He's the man who single-handedly won World War II. The man who always comes top of those 'vote for Britain's greatest ever prime minister' polls. Damn it, he comes top of the 'vote for the greatest Briton ever' polls! There are mementoes to Winston Churchill across Britain and the world. Nevertheless, the good people of Woodford do not always show their love for their local MP (1945–64). Graffiti often appears on David McFall's 1959 bronze in Woodford Green in a way that would be impossible on a bust of, say, Kim Jong-un in Pyongyang.

The statue was even the symbol of the local council, Redbridge, during the 2012 London Olympic Games. Yet the locked down public gave it a bit of grief in June 2020 at a time when metal tributes to major figures in history – basically anyone to the right of Jeremy Corbyn – were bearing the brunt of rampaging politically correct gangs. After Churchill was defaced that month, local police patrols were increased, and the statue was cleaned and restored. Then council leader Jas Athwal announced with gross insensitivity that the council would be reviewing the appropriateness of local monuments and statues. Remembering his public responsibility, he then U-turned and urged people not to react in anger.

Winston Churchill started his parliamentary career as a Tory in Oldham in 1900 but within a few years had crossed the floor to the Liberals over the issue of free trade. He later returned to the Tories over the same issue. By the 1930s, he was in the political wilderness, but returned to prominence as Britain edged closer to war, and took over as PM from Neville Chamberlain in 1940. In one of the most remarkable political events in British history, he lost the immediate post-war general election in 1945 as the public chose to support Labour's plans for social improvement via the National Health Service and mass nationalisation.

Address Woodford Green (the A1199), Woodford, IG8 9HJ | Getting there Underground to Woodford (Central Line) | Hours Accessible 24 hours | Tip Winston Churchill was also a tireless amateur painter, but none of his works are on display at the William Morris Gallery in nearby Walthamstow, dedicated to the great Victorian polymath.

70 The Gypsy Stone
Gypsies, champs and leaves

Rodney 'Gipsy' Smith was known as the gypsies' champ. Born in 1860 in a Romany bender tent here in Epping Forest, now marked with this commemorative stone, he became a vociferous evangelist and an early member of the Salvation Army.

Smith was self-educated. His parents sold baskets and clothes pegs from their vardo. His mother died when he was a child. Although his father was in and out of jail, Smith heard the gospel from a prison chaplain, and he and his brothers were converted at a mission meeting. They even visited John Bunyan's home in Bedford. They took their gypsy encampment to the Liverpool International Exhibition.

He taught himself to read and write and began to sing hymns to the people he met. At a Christian Mission in London, Smith met William Booth, founder of the Salvation Army, who groomed him as a street corner preacher. This was at a time when social changes were threatening the gypsy way of life with enclosures of common land, and the authorities were trying to influence them into abandoning their lifestyle. An 1878 Act of Parliament saved Epping Forest from enclosure, and preserved the huge woodland area for the nation, but ironically barred gypsies from camping there.

Smith and his party travelled the world on evangelistic crusades, drawing thousands and visiting Romany encampments. During the Great War he worked with the YMCA ministering to the British troops in France. Smith died on board the *Queen Mary* while sailing from New York to Florida, aged 87. The story wasn't over. In 1991, two girls claimed to have been raped on this spot by their parents and a descendent of Rodney Smith as part of Satanic rites that included the killing and eating of babies. The court threw it out for lack of evidence.

This granite stone contains a carving of a traditional gypsy wagon. Below is a plaque containing information about Smith's life and achievements.

Address 100 yards north-west of the junction of Woodford New Road and the A 406, Walthamstow Country Park, Woodford, IG8 9NU | Getting there See address, above; Woodford tube station is 1.5 miles to the north-east | Hours Accessible 24 hours | Tip Explore this cut-off southern north-south stretch of Epping Forest, a surprise find in an overdeveloped area.

71 Magnificent Maldon
Worth its salt

Maldon is often mentioned in those 'best secret town in England' awards and it's no surprise why. Here, nine miles east of Chelmsford, with no railway to attract the commuters, you can find charm, heritage and a dozen vineyards. Picturesque cottages bustle for attention by the glorious River Blackwater, Hythe Quay is home to a number of old Thames barges, and at Heybridge Basin, the 13-mile Chelmer and Blackwater Navigation joins the Blackwater Estuary at an antiquated wooden lock. There are old churches, antique stores, Mrs Salisbury's Famous Tea Rooms and miniature cake shops (the cakes are mini, not the shops). Jeez, even the Wetherspoons is attractive.

Maldon has lovely weather, with hardly any rain, although it can be a bit windy when 'Zephirus eek with his sweete breeth' blows in from the North Sea. Shakespeare visited with the King's Men in 1603, fleeing the Plague. But it's also the kind of area where it's no surprise to discover that an escaped emu called Farage recently legged it down a snow-covered high street at 30 mph.

But Maldon's main contribution to the British economy is its sea salt, renowned worldwide. The Domesday Book of 1086 lists 45 working saltpans in the town, four owned by Edward the Confessor, and the ancient art of salt panning is still alive on the Essex coast. Salt panning involves boiling seawater to form crystal flakes. An ingenious procedure removes the nasty bits of pollution, fish poo and the like in a process that has remained little changed since Roman times. This takes place, romantically, at spring tide, full Moon and new Moon when thousands of gallons of seawater are extracted as the water floods the rich saltmarshes. There are no additives to the product whose delicate, slightly sweet taste is beloved by chefs and home cooks alike. 'It's an absolutely pure salt that tastes of the sea,' says the great Delia Smith.

Address Maldon, CM9 | Getting there Maldon is south-east of the A 12 between Broomfield and Witham | Tip The delightful Farmers Yard at 140 High Street is one of the smallest pubs in Essex.

72 Oldest UK Battlefield

Byrhtnoth the Vanquished

Forget Battle in Sussex and the Battle of Hastings. Maldon, eight miles east of Chelmsford, is Britain's oldest battlefield, dating back to the year A.D. 991 when it witnessed Essex's unsuccessful defence against the Viking hordes. Indeed, it is the only pre-1066 English battlefield that can be accurately located.

Just to make sure no one misses the story, here is John Doubleday's statue of the main man, Byrhtnoth, killed at the battle. It went up at the end of the Maldon Promenade Walk in October 2006 and faces both the National Trust-owned battle site and Northey Island. The event is also marked in the Old English poem 'The Battle of Maldon' and a play by Tolkein.

Byrhtnoth came of good stock. He was married to Ælfflæd, sister of the dowager Queen Æthelflæd of Damerham and related by marriage to King Edgar (England's king A.D. 959–975). The name comes from the Old English *beorht* (bright) and *noð* (courage), thereby reminding lovers of ancient English history of the long-lost letter ð – *eth*. Byrhtnoth was over 6 feet tall, 60 years old, with 'swan-white hair'. He was experienced at thwarting Viking raiders, but military experts believe his decision to allow the Vikings to move to a better position on the day was fatal. It took three men to kill him, one of whom almost severed Byrhtnoth's arm in doing so. The warrior was buried in Ely Abbey and his widow gave Ely a long-lost tapestry, like Bayeux's. Unhelpfully, his remains have been moved and reburied three times.

Viking raiders used nearby Northey Island as their base. For those who would like to appreciate what conditions might have been like for the doughty Danes, take a day trip (by arrangement) to this uninhabited island and contemplate. These days, Northey is a peaceful wilderness and bird watchers' paradise, home to redshank, plover and thousands of Brent geese. No Vikings have been seen recently.

Address Promenade Park, Maldon, CM9 5UR | **Getting there** This is an area devoid of main roads and railway. Head east from Maldon to the River Chelmer, en route to Northey Island. | **Hours** Accessible 24 hours | **Tip** Head into Maldon itself to explore the town and espy the Moot Hall, a Grade I-listed municipal building, built in 1420 by wealthy Essex MP Robert D'Arcy.

73 — A House for Essex
Fairy eccentric

Stunning and spectacular, here is Grayson Perry's remarkable House for Essex. It was created as a 'chapel to the history of his home county of Essex' designed by the crossdressing, Turner Prize-winning artist himself along with Charles Holland for Alain de Botton's Living Architecture project.

The house is clad in ceramic tiles and has a four-part roof topped with large cast-aluminium sculptures. 'It's a hybrid building; part house and part gallery,' says Holland. According to Grayson Perry: 'The idea behind this project relates to buildings put up as memorials to loved ones, to follies, to eccentric home-built structures, to shrines, lighthouses and fairytales. I wanted it to be very small and very rich,' but he has added that 'without Holland's intervention it would've looked like the set from *Game of Thrones*.'

Outside, the house is set in a romantic landscape overlooking the Stour Estuary. The copper-clad roof is based on medieval stave churches. Inside, the house is an eccentric's delight, decorated with interior balconies, beautiful tapestries and specially-commissioned artworks, including mosaic floors, pots and delicate furnishings. The building is split into four parts that increase in scale, like a retractable telescope.

The contents depict the life of a fictional Essex woman, Julie Cope, who is represented iconographically as a saint. A motorbike hoisted up on the ceiling of the chapel recalls her collision with a curry delivery driver that saw Julie meet her end, and a tombstone in the front garden marks her final resting place. The reactionary local press initially slammed the property as 'little more than a conceptual holiday home' and a 'gingerbread house'. They've since jumped on the bandwagon.

To experience the concept of this real-life artefact, you can enter a ballot to win the chance to stay. Understandably, tickets are at a premium.

Address Black Boy Lane, Wrabness, Manningtree, CO11 2TP, +44 (0)203 488 1584, www.living-architecture.co.uk | **Getting there** Train to Wrabness; by car, take the A 120 towards Harwich and head north a couple of miles east of Wix | **Hours** See website for latest booking information; tickets are occasionally available without the need to enter a ballot | **Tip** A little south of the station is John Drury's rare and antiquarian bookshop, for more everyday culture.

74 The Manningtree Tree
Old Knobbley

This is one hell of a tree! Old Knobbley is one of the oldest oaks in England, famed for its twisted and gnarled appearance, its wide branches spread out, welcoming all who come to gaze at its majesty.

Old Knobbley is more than 13 feet tall and almost three times as wide. It has somehow survived lightning, fire, hornets and most awfully of all, witches who used to hide within its cracks and crevices from the incorrigible Witchfinder General Matthew Hopkins (see ch. 26) who operated villainously locally. Hopkins owned the local Thorn Inn, where he 'examined' his first witch. He was probably responsible for the deaths of 300 women between 1644 and 1646. At the same location, heretic Thomas Osmond had been burned in June 1555. The tree provided succour to troops during World War II when the army cut down its neighbours to build wooden huts for soldiers.

Manningtree managed a mention in Shakespeare, who passed through as a young actor, thanks to its livestock. In *Henry IV Part I*, Prince Henry jests, talking about Falstaff, 'There is a devil haunts thee in the likeness of an old fat man… that roasted Manningtree ox with the pudding in his belly.' At the local fair an entire ox would be roasted, stuffed with black pudding made thereof. But maybe Shakespeare didn't really exist as such and he was actually a cipher for courtier Edward de Vere who was born locally at Hedingham Castle. Either way, Manningtree institutions have long used the ox as a symbol of local bovine pride. Gone is the Church of St Michael, demolished in 1965. Its Constable painting, *The Ascension*, is now in Dedham Church.

Manningtree is said to be England's smallest town. At high tide, the town is only 20 hectares in size and the recent population number was just 700. In 2009, plans were proposed to merge Manningtree with its surrounding villages, Mistley and Lawford, but this was later scrapped.

Address Gamekeepers' Pond, Mistley Compendium, Manningtree, CO11 2NL | **Getting there** The tree is a few yards south-west of the junction of Shrublands Road and the B 1352; train to Mistley, then a 10-minute walk | **Hours** Accessible 24 hours | **Tip** The former fire station on High Street displays an iron cast of the Manningtree Ox, marking the town's Shakespeare connection. Hanging inside the belly of the sculpture is a large, golden ball that represents the black pudding.

75 Twin Towers of Mistley

Didn't there used to be a church here?

Robert Adam, the greatest of Georgian architects, didn't build many churches, and of these, the Church of St Mary the Virgin at Mistley near Manningtree, all that's left are the towers – the church has disappeared.

Adam was commissioned by Richard Rigby of Mistley Hall to build the church. His father had trousered a small fortune at the time of the South Sea speculation, and Rigby himself made a mint when George III appointed him Paymaster General of the Forces in 1768. At that time Rigby was planning to turn Mistley into a fashionable spa, and Adam was to design a saltwater bath by the river. Instead, in 1776, the architect started work on the church.

His design was unusual – towers at the east and west ends and semi-circular porticos on the north and south sides influenced by Roman tombs. Unfortunately, the scheme didn't work out as planned, and the main body of the church was demolished in 1870. Nevertheless, these gorgeous towers of rendered brickwork with Portland stone decoration have been preserved as a landmark.

Mistley is a village 11 miles north-east of Colchester by the Stour Estuary. In the 1640s it was the home of one of the worst figures in Essex history, Matthew Hopkins, the Witchfinder General. He was buried in the graveyard of the medieval church, only the porch of which survives. By the time Adam was working on the church there was much trade, thanks to Rigby's work on improving the nearby port. One well-heeled visitor, Maximilien de Lazowski, noted how 'Newcastle ships bring coal, which is either distributed by cart into Essex or Suffolk or carried on upriver by barge to Sudbury. The whole neighbourhood brings its corn here to be embarked or stored for the London markets.' After that, nothing much ever happened here apart from Mistley being the location of a Cold War nuclear bunker control room in 1951 for the atomic war that never happened.

Address Church Hall, The Walls, Mistley, Manningtree, CO11 1ET | Getting there Train to Mistley, then a 10-minute walk; by car, take the B 1352 east to the river estuary | Hours Viewable from the outside 24 hours; you can request a key for the towers from the nearby Mistley Thorn Hotel in the High Street between 10am and 4pm | Tip In the churchyard you can find several 18th-century monuments, among them a curious black granite Egyptian-style mausoleum to the Norman family.

76 — Shakespeare Tempest Isle

Such stuff as dreams are not made on

Twice a day remote Mersea, the most easterly populated island in England, endures a high tide that covers the only road in and out, and prevents anyone from entering or leaving. So it was a fitting setting for *The Tempest*, Shakespeare's 1611 play. *The Tempest* deals with magic, betrayal and revenge, is set on a remote island, and features the sorcerer Prospero; his daughter, Miranda; a savage monster figure of a servant, Caliban; and a flighty spirit, Ariel.

Mersea is just one of a host of small Essex islands caused by the gradual encroachment of the waters. It lies nine miles south of Colchester and is surrounded by the mouths of the Rivers Blackwater and Colne. The watery name comes from the Old English *meresig* – 'island of the pool'. There is evidence of pre-Roman activity with the remains of Celtic salt workings. The Romans, based at their capital, nearby Colchester, used it as a holiday resort. Industry has always been fishing, and Mersea is famed for its oysters, particularly those from the Pacific, which haven't swum here but were introduced recently.

Of the 320 soldiers from Mersea who went to fight in the Great War, as many as 50 lost their lives. Troops took over Mersea during World War II and heavily fortified the place, as can be seen in a number of observation posts. The island was also used for evacuees from London. Mersea suffered from the severe winter of 1947 and the flooding of 1953, but on 4 June, 2012, as part of the Queen's Diamond Jubilee celebrations, the island declared independence from Britain, just for the day. Anyone travelling to the island had to pay 50p for a passport, the proceeds of which went towards war military charities.

Mersea is the setting for Margery Allingham's first novel, *Blackkerchief Dick*, from 1923, published when she was 19, which she initially claimed was based on a story she had heard during a séance.

Address Mersea Island, CO5 8DE | **Getting there** Follow signs to Mersea Island B 1025. There is no bridge to the island. Visitors and residents have to rely on the Strood, and no one is sure whether the Strood is road or stream. | **Hours** You'll need to check tide times before attempting to cross – www.tidetimes.org.uk/west-mersea-tide-times | **Tip** Head for Monkey Beach where not just children but explorers of all ages can set about discovering the network of tiny creeks and boardwalks.

77 Greensted-juxta-Ongar
UK's oldest wooden church

Greensted's church is believed to be the oldest existing wooden building in Europe, although only a few sections of its original wooden structure remain. What has survived are the oak walls, which might be remnants of a palisade church made of timber logs forced into the ground, dating back to the mid-ninth century. There are also 51 visible timber planks dating from about the year 1060.

The building's full title is the Church of St Andrew, Greensted-juxta-Ongar and it still holds services. Construction probably began just after Cedd began converting the East Saxons in the year A.D. 654. Archaeological digs found two simple wooden buildings under the present chancel floor from that period. The nave is made of large split oak trunks, as was the traditional way of building at that time. The white weatherboarded tower is 17th century. In 1990 the church was stabilised, and in 2005 the spire was covered in oak.

The body of King Edmund the Martyr of East Anglia, killed by the Danes in battle in the year A.D. 869 rested within in the year 1013, on its way to burial at Bury St Edmunds, and there are tributes to St Edmund, England's first patron saint, inside. The church also contains a leper squint, a small opening through the oak wall that allowed lepers, who were not allowed inside the church, to mix with the public and receive blessings from the priest.

The church lies a mile west of Chipping Ongar and is surrounded by farms whose tenancies were granted to some of the early 19th-century Tolpuddle Martyrs, trade unionists convicted and transported to Australia who then returned to Britain. Indeed, one of the martyrs, James Brine, married Elizabeth Standfield at Greensted Church in 1839. They had 11 children and Brine lived to 90, dying in 1902. He built a log house that still stands and is now the only building associated with the Martyrs left standing in Britain.

Address Church Lane, Ongar, CM5 9LD, +44 (0)1277 532770, www.greenstedchurch.org.uk | Getting there By car, take the M11 to Junction 7, then head east along the A 414 to Chipping Ongar and take the B 184 south | Hours Open most days 10am – 4pm, 6pm in summer; guided tours can be arranged | Tip Two more excellent churches can be found nearby: St Martin's Chipping Ongar and St Peter's, Shelley.

78 Most Obscure Tube Station

'Theydon Bois on guitar'

It's been a standing joke in east London and west Essex for decades. Bored kids at half-term would make the day-long (it felt like that) journey from inhabited areas of the capital to Ongar station just for the *craic*, enticed by the strange name and the fact that nobody knew where it was. When they got there, in pre-ticket machine times, they would tell the ticket collector they had got on one stop before (the equally obscure Blake Hall) rather than at West Kensington miles and miles away.

The station was opened in 1865, long before the Tube was invented, as part of the Great Eastern Railway to take farm produce and the occasional commuter into central London. Although the station is located in Chipping Ongar, clearly the railway authorities couldn't get to grips with the whole name and dubbed it simply as 'Ongar'. It became part of London Transport in 1949 when the Central Line started to be extended so far eastwards the public assumed it would soon make Clacton. What a shock for masticating bovine quadrupeds to see tube trains passing by as they munched their way through the meadows.

Just to add to the quaintness, the new line was single track and sported steam trains, electricity not quite having stretched that far in Essex. And to add to the discomfort, trains from London could only make it to Epping, so there had to be a shuttle service to reach Ongar. There was method to the madness. The buffers at Ongar station became Point Zero from which distances on the London Underground would be measured.

Over the years, London Transport kept running down the service until the final cut came on 30 September, 1994. A privately owned Epping to Ongar Railway opened in 2004, struggled on to 2007, and then reopened in 2012 with steam trains. Sadly, the Mayor of London did not identify Ongar as central to the new Crossrail.

Address Station Approach, Chipping Ongar, CM5 9BN | **Getting there** The station is just south of the A 414 in Chipping Ongar | **Hours** See steam railway website www.eorailway.co.uk/visit for train timetables | **Tip** In his book *How to Be a Complete Bastard*, the comedian Ade Edmondson suggested people could measure up to the cuss in the title by telling tourists that all of London's main tourist attractions were within walking distance of Ongar station.

79___Bull's Folly

Mum and dad: is this right?

It's one of the weirdest structures in Essex: part industrial chimney, fully folly, dominating the small village of Pentlow near Braintree. Bull's Folly, octagonal and of red brick, stands 95 feet in the garden of a rectory. It went up in 1859 thanks to the Rev Edward Bull in memory of his parents, the Rev John and Mrs Margaret Bull, 'on a spot that they loved so well'. Another motive was Bull's rivalry with his friend the Rev John Foster, Rector of the neighbouring village of Foxearth. Foster had built a 130-foot spire at the top of his church tower, so Bull had to save face. His tower is smaller but more conspicuous and unusual. Vengeance came in 1948 when Foster's tower was destroyed during a thunderstorm.

The brick is banded with diapered crosses and diamonds, with the date – 1859 – prominently set above the door. Further up are the initials 'Aci' picked out in dark blue brick and standing for Anno Christi, rather than the more usual Anno Domini. Windows in the sides light the oaken 114-step spiral staircase. The only problem was, would the staircase rot away as you climbed? Would you step on a dead rat? At the top are reassuring views of scores of phone masts as well as 41 churches, 60 windmills, two castles and several large halls and estates.

They used to say, tug on the old bell pull and far away in the depths of the house a cold clinical clang would be heard but no one would answer. No wonder it was called the most terrifying tower in Britain. The good reverend left Pentlow to become rector four miles away and in 1865 built himself a new rectory, which burnt down in 1941, around the time that Bull's Folly had its uses as a lookout tower in World War II.

In recent years, restoration has started to eradicate the decrepitude. The Tower is now used as a venue for conferences and wedding receptions. A Union Jack flies on great occasions.

Address Lion Road, Glemsford, Pentlow, CO10 7JN | **Getting there** By car, take the A 134 to Sudbury and head west | **Hours** Viewable from the outside only | **Tip** Head to nearby Sudbury and soak in the vistas. Here was the birthplace of the great 18th-century artist Thomas Gainsborough whose landscapes inspired an even greater local artist, Constable.

80 Keith Flint's Pub
Mine's a firestarter!

It was one of the greatest music tragedies of recent years: the prema-
ture death through suicide in 2019 of Keith Flint, ferocious frontman
for The Prodigy, raucous, rebellious ravers of the electro scene and
purveyors of some of the most exciting music of the 1990s.

The Prodigy were formed in Braintree, Essex, as an electro dance
band, mixing breakbeats with fierce pounding rave-inspired rhythms
and a viciously uncompromising punk ethos, bringing classic but
unknown reggae, such as Max Romeo's 'Out of Space' to the masses.
They were mean, they were marvellous, and Keith had mad staring
eyes, sticky out spiky hair, and more piercings than there were body
parts to pierce. Somewhat controversial was their 1997 single 'Smack
My Bitch Up', clearly not the kind of ditty you might play to the
local vicar when he comes to tea. More incendiary was the earlier
'Firestarter', content obvious, video frightening, the best 'Hey, Hey,
Hey' single since T. Rex's 'Solid Gold Easy Action'. It caused much
spluttering in the House of Commons.

Keith Flint took over the Leather Bottle pub near Chelmsford in 2014. Patrons were surprised to find the landlord a mild-
mannered charmer with an entertaining personality who existed off
stage and screen, and even took part in the local park run. When
people complained about the pub on TripAdvisor, Keith would
write back personally. One moaned that 'the radio was playing as
background music'. Keith, as comical as ever, replied: 'If I'd been
in there on the real ales or had a couple of Jaegers, the radio will
creep up.'

Best of all, Keith placed a 'Firestarter' jar in the pub and made
customers put a pound in every time they referenced his hit single
while he was lighting the pub's fire. Two pounds presumably if you
called him a 'trouble starter, punkin' instigator, fear addicted, danger
illustrated, twisted firestarter'.

Address Leather Bottle, The Street, Pleshey, CM3 1HG, +44 (0)1245 237291, www.facebook.com/theleatherbottlepleshey | Getting there Tiny Pleshey is eight miles north of Chelmsford | Hours Mon 12.15–11pm, Tue–Sat 12.15pm–midnight, Sun noon–midnight | Tip For a more sedate bibulous experience, head east to Great Waltham and the sophisticated award-winning Galvin Green Man, one of the oldest pubs in Essex.

81__ The Pink Toothbrush

'I'm a pink toothbrush, you're a blue toothbrush'

It's Essex's best-known and corniest nightclub. Some say it's the UK's longest running alternative nightclub. Boy George and Culture Club might have made their debut here, but no one's absolutely sure. De La Soul, all the way from Long Island, and Ice T, all the way from hustling on the street, have appeared, as have Soft Cell, Blur and Radiohead. There have been DJ sets from the cast of the Inbetweeners. Essex's greatest group, Depeche Mode (or is it The Prodigy, or Procol Harum?) played here so many times it seemed they had a residency. The clientele were Goths and punks, but there were also celebrity visits from comedian Phill Jupitus, the spoken word poet Scroobius Pip, and members of the Mode and Culture Club. Pre covid, the club was full to capacity and queues stretched down the street at weekends.

The newspapers often ran pieces on why the club was so successful as rivals fell. In 2019 Stu Whiffen, the Brush's promoter and occasional DJ, explained that loyalty to staff and its customers played a big part. 'We've often had other venues put on indie nights. There was a very successful one at Club Art called Rage. In a lot of mainstream clubland there's a lot of competition, but we're not competitive. We've often found people outside flyering for their own indie night, and we say: "It's cold out there, come in and flyer in the corridor."'

Originally, in 1979, the club was Crocs as two live beasts were sleepily on display in a cage. But the club should have been named Alli's or Alligators, for the crocs were alligators. They were eventually given to Colchester Zoo, after which the club was renamed after Max Bygraves' best-known song, 'You're a Pink Toothbrush', which describes a meeting between two toothbrushes of different sexually recognised colours. The club now hosts its own radio station showcasing alternative music with appropriate chat and bants,

Address 19–23 High Street, Rayleigh, SS6 7EW, +44 (0)1268 770003,
www.pinktoothbrush.co.uk | Getting there Train to Rayleigh; by car, take the A127 to
Rayleigh and then head north on the A129 | Hours Fri & Sat 10pm–3am | Tip Stumble
out of the Brush as dawn breaks and head to Bellingham Lane to admire the majesty of the
Rayleigh Windmill.

82 — Osea Island
Exclusively yours

Imagine your very own island in the sun; well, in the middle of the River Blackwater Estuary, 10 miles east of Chelmsford, almost in the sea, with a lot of wind and fog, and just one road in and out helpfully built by the Romans, accessible only for four hours a day.

Record producer Nigel Frieda doesn't have to, 'cause he owns it, all half a square mile of it. Frieda, founder of the Sugababes pop combo, who runs London's Matrix Studio, bought the whole thing for £6 million in 2000. Rumours soon spread in tabloid land that the singer Rhianna would be crossing the water to record her ninth album here as the state-of-the-art studio has its own gym, cinema and pool alongside quaint little cottages for her entourage. Mere mortals can book a stay, but there aren't many amenities other than delightful wading birds.

Osea is popular with film companies. The 1979 picture *Black Island*, shot on the island, featured two young castaways captured by escaped convicts and their attempt at escaping. Osea was owned in the late 19th century by Frederick Charrington of the famous brewing family, and there he set up home to a Temperance Society, and built a drug and alcohol rehabilitation centre where one of the inmates, it is believed, was the controversial artist and prime Ripper suspect Walter Sickert. The facility was revived earlier this century with a clinic visited by Amy Winehouse.

Things are changing on Osea. Before 2004 there were only a few residents, including a painter, a photographer and a philosopher. However, great things are afoot. A Scottish company has been talking about launching transport on a, wait for it, seaplane, not seen since the 1950s, so that well-heeled travellers can board in the capital, sip cocktails in Zoot Suits or New Look dresses and chat about the latest crazy Charleston-styled dance, alighting on Osea 20 minutes later.

Address Maldon, CM9 8UH | Getting there There isn't much choice other than taking the B 1026 east from Heybridge | Hours Check www.tidetimes.org.uk/osea-island-tide-times for tidal charts showing the low tide 4-hour window; river taxis are bookable during high tide for the 10-minute trip | Tip Head back to the mainland east to delightful St Lawrence with its glorious sea front walks but reminders of difficult times with its flood wall and World War II pillboxes.

83 Georgia Founder's Grave

An old stone vault that keeps Georgia on our minds

Here in Cranham, the easternmost village of any London borough, but what should still be the Romford Rural District of Essex if the authorities hadn't messed up the boundaries, is the grave of James Edward Oglethorpe (1696–1785).

Oglethorpe founded the US state of Georgia, and lies in a vault beneath the chancel floor of All Saints' church. He was the owner of Cranham Hall Manor, and after Oxford joined the Austrian army as a mercenary to fight the Turks. His experience working on prison reforms gave him the idea of founding a new colony in America for London's indebted prisoners and persecuted Protestant sects. Thirty-five families left Gravesend, opposite Essex's Tilbury, in November 1732 on the ship *Anne* and arrived at Charleston two months later. That year, the territory became the Province of Georgia, named after the British king, George II. Initially its purpose was to protect South Carolina from the Spanish invading through Florida. When war broke out between England and Spain in 1739, he led a vigorous defence of the territory.

Oglethorpe imposed strict laws that many disagreed with, such as banning of alcohol. Unusually for the time, he opposed slavery and therefore set up smallholdings rather than large plantations. The ban on slavery was lifted in 1751 due to envy of the financial bonanza of slavery in the Carolinas and the colony came under the British Crown. In 1788, Georgia became an American state.

Obscure Cranham was first recorded in 1086 as Cravoho and this church as All Saints' in 1254. In 1958, choir stalls and an altar rail were donated by the National Society of Colonial Dames of the USA. The woodwork contains the arms of the State of Georgia and of Oglethorpe himself. The man himself is lucky to still be in Cranham, given that Oglethorpe University in Atlanta asked for his remains to be sent over there in 1925 but were turned down.

Address The Chase, Cranham, Upminster, RM14 3YB, +44 (0)1708 228308, www.allsaintscranham.co.uk | Getting there Train to Upminster, then a 25-minute walk; by car, take the B 187 east from Upminster | Hours Viewable from the outside 24 hours and inside during services | Tip More heritage can be savoured in Upminster's Tithe Barn Museum of Nostalgia.

84 Air Control Tower Des Res

Not such a plane property

'Control, this is Saffron Walden. Don't land here. It's not an aircraft control tower any more. It's my house!'

This is one of the most unusual properties in Essex, where a one-time aircraft control tower has been turned into a remarkable residency. Let's face it, your average home does not have such commanding views of the surrounding countryside, nor a ground floor with duty pilot's rest room, meteorological office and switch room, a first-floor control room and signals office, and an open-plan living room fitted with bespoke rosewood cupboards.

What was Hadstock Control Tower was built in 1942 by the Air Ministry's Directorate of Works and Buildings. It stands on the former Little Walden airfield from where the 409th Bombardment Group flew missions to support the US Third Army as it advanced from France into Germany during World War II. Saffron Walden saw one hundred bombing raids during the war, their pilots engaged in dive-bombing missions to attack airfields, marshalling yards, missile sites, industrial areas, ordnance depots, oil refineries, trains and highways. It was also used by the RAF and US Air Force in the run-up to D-Day.

The Control Tower is one of more than 150 examples of a 1930s design that arose when the air force realised the need to incorporate the very latest measures for dealing with dispersal and shelter of aircraft from attack. Of these, 82 survive. This one went on sale in 2002 for £775,000 after being converted into a stylish home. It is the best preserved of its kind and was the inspiration for the deserted control tower in Anthony Asquith's film *The Way to the Stars* (1945), which depicts life on a British bomber base from the early days of the Battle of Britain to the arrival of the Americans. Love and disillusionment feature heavily.

Address Hadstock, Saffron Walden, CB 21 4PA | Getting there Just east off the B 1052 between Hadstock and Little Walden | Hours Viewable from the outside only | Tip Essex abounds with aerodromes and airfields. Head south to Andrewsfield Aerodrome for necessary flying lessons after all that control tower gubbins.

85 Temple of Concord
Arrive before you leave

Sir John Griffin Griffin, the tautologically titled late 18th-century field marshal (so good they named him twice) built this Classically-styled Corinthian structure in the grounds of his Audley End mansion in 1790–91 to celebrate George III's recovery from insanity.

Audley End's Temple of Concord is modelled on the original that was built in Rome from around 360 B.C. and dedicated to Concordia, the Roman goddess of harmony. The Essex version is surrounded by a ha-ha ring (no laughing in the cheap seats) and sits near a palatial mansion, one of the finest Jacobean houses in England, built on the site of Walden Abbey, a Benedictine monastery dissolved in 1538.

Forty years later, Queen Elizabeth stopped at Audley during her Summer Progress, a journey through the country seeking out scholarship and theatrical performances. During one session, Gabriel Harvey, Professor of Rhetoric at Cambridge, wrote a most interesting missive to her courtier, Edward de Vere, 17th Earl of Oxford. 'Mars lives in thy tongue, Minerva strengthens thy right hand, Bellona reigns in thy body, within thee burns the fire of Mars. Thine eyes flash fire, thy countenance *shakes a spear.*'

These lines have fuelled hundreds of years of conspiracy theories alleging that the Earl of Oxford wrote the plays attributed to one William Shakespeare (even though they were most probably written by Francis Bacon).

The original house was demolished by Thomas Howard, First Earl of Suffolk, but reworked in a grand style for entertaining James I. Too grand. Suffolk was found guilty of embezzlement and sent to the Tower. A huge fine securing his release did not prevent his dying in disgrace at Charing Cross in 1626. Samuel Pepys visited Audley End and noted in his diary for Monday 27 February, 1659 that he was excitingly shown the wine cellar 'where we drank a most admirable drink, a health to the King'.

Address Parterre Garden, off London Road, CB 11 4JF, in the grounds of grand Audley End House, one of the largest mansions in England; a visit to the house is a must | Getting there Train to Audley End, then a walk; Audley End Road, Audley End, Saffron Walden CB 11 4JF | Hours Gardens daily 10am–5pm; house daily 10.30am–4pm | Tip Explore Saffron Walden itself, cited in the *Sunday Times* 'Best Places to Live in the UK 2021' due to its 'timeless good looks'.

86 Town of Mazes

No need for a labyrinth when the universe is one

There's little more annoying for the intrepid *flâneur* than trying to eradicate yourself out of a maze with only seconds left to get the last bus. Well, in Saffron Walden, the delightful market town in north Essex, there's a whole series of them, in enough shapes and sizes to warm the bones of even the late Jorge Luis Borges, legendary Argentinian author and obsessive of labyrinths.

There's the Hedge Maze, which is situated in the Victorian garden at Bridge End. By the end of World War II it had fallen into neglect, but was restored in the 1980s when the paths and banks were reconstructed and more than a thousand yews were planted.

Near the ruins of the 12th-century castle built by Geoffrey de Mandeville, First Earl of Essex, is the Turf Maze, the largest of its kind in the world, and one of only eight survivors, the design taken from the famous Chartres Cathedral in France. It is more properly a labyrinth, as there is only one route and no false turns. No one knows why it was built.

Medieval labyrinths are associated with religious penances and fertility rites, but they were also used for games, and bets would be placed on the outcome of races to the centre. The Guy Fawkes festivities of 1823 were so rowdy that an ash tree in the middle of the maze was burnt to the ground.

Looking for more twists and turns? There's a modern paved labyrinth in the Jubilee Garden and the Sun Maze Sculpture is in the Fry Art Gallery. But Saffron Walden has much agricultural history. Political journalist Colin Welch, who spent the 1945 general election canvassing here for the Tory grandee R. A. Butler, saw a Labour rival approach a yeoman farmer leaning on the proverbial five-bar gate sucking a straw and tell him it was in the class interests of people such as him to vote for Mr Attlee. 'Ma'am,' the yeoman replied, 'Oi've made moi poile, an' yo can go to bu***ry.'

Address Various – the Tourist Information Centre produces a useful guide to the mazes: visitsaffronwalden.gov.uk/wp-content/uploads/2019/10/Saffron-Walden-Mazes.pdf | **Getting there** Saffron Walden lies at the junction of the B 1052 and the B 184; train to Audley End | **Tip** For further spiritual reflection, head to the town's Catholic church, Our Lady of Compassion, on Castle Street, created in 1906 from a 16th-century barn.

87 — Ministry of Defence Beach
Danger of death – really!

It's so tempting. Take the train to the furthest eastern edge of the known world – Shoeburyness – and head north along the beach, only to find that the men from the ministry don't want you there. Here, on a strategic site, which came in very useful during two world wars given its clear sight lines to Europe, is a private Ministry of Defence artillery range.

The warnings are clear: *The site is a former LIVE weapons testing and proving ground. The beach is still owned by the Ministry of Defence, therefore take heed of all notices posted around the site. Do not pick up, kick or remove any metallic or any other objects from the site, failure to heed the advice could result in death or injury to yourself or others.*

Get to know the signage. There are 21 red flags to mark the area subject to the Range. Some are visible from afar and others from the Thames Estuary and River Crouch. These red flags at full mast indicate that the Range is active and that bye-laws are in force. Enter then at your peril! When Yellow Diamonds are mounted on the yard arm of Red Flag poles, the public may occupy the whole of Shoeburyness' east beach out to the yellow buoy line. But when the Yellow Diamonds are lowered, entry to the beach and sands area is out.

Located on raised land at the mouth of the Thames Estuary, Shoeburyness has had strategic importance since prehistoric times. Ramparts protected an Iron Age settlement, and parts survive, together with evidence of round houses, ditches and post holes. The Romans built a fort here that was attacked by the natives in A.D. 50. The military arrived at this excellently secluded position in 1849 when the government Board of Ordnance bought the land as a practice range, as Woolwich Common was too near the people, and soon began testing weapons when the Crimean War broke out. You can always visit in a suit of armour.

Address North-east of High Street, Shoeburyness, SS3 9SR | **Getting there** Shoeburyness is at the eastern end of the A13; train to Shoeburyness | **Hours** Having read all the warnings above, if you're still unsure of what areas you can and can't visit, contact +44 (0)1702 383211 | **Tip** Shoeburyness has a rare mention in Ian Dury's 1977 song 'Billericay Dickie', where he sings about a 'lovely old toerag, kindly Charmaine Shag from Shoeburyness'.

88 Port of London Marker

That's your limit!

Out in the sands in Southend, due north of Yantlet Creek and south of Chalkwell Avenue, standing proud and glorious, is an obelisky lump of stone. Some say that from the shore, it looks like a mysterious ruin of an ancient civilisation, but it's simply the Crow Stone of Chalkwell and it marks the furthest the Port of London Authority has jurisdiction over the water, even though it's some 30 miles from the old port.

The Crow Stone went up, or rather was stuck down, in 1837, replacing a smaller stone dating from 1755, which is now in Southend's Priory Park. Historians believe there has been a marker on this site since 1285. It's not alone. On the southern side of the estuary, on the Isle of Grain in Kent, is its brother, the London Stone. The line between the Crow Stone and the London Stone is known as the Yantlet Line. Essex's Crow Stone is the looker.

Next to the Crow Stone are two Victorian pathways in the mud made of raised areas of pebbles with low rotten wooden fences of elm and decking wide enough to allow horse and cart to travel. They go down into deeper water that becomes the Ray, a tributary of the Thames that flows between Hadleigh and Benfleet. There are various explanations of the pathways' purpose. They were for boats serving the Leigh oyster industry; maybe during World War II they were used for wheeling out anti-aircraft guns during low tide to get closer to Nazi planes flying down the Thames to bomb London. Or perhaps they were to allow troops to board ships headed for the D-Day landings. Either that or the paths were for sewage.

Despite being so close to the Kent coast, Essex's Southend has little connection with its neighbour. There are no ferry services, possibly because opposite this great seaside resort are the isolated Isle of Grain and Sheppey, whereas the similar Margate in Kent is about 25 miles south-east.

Address On the beach, along Chalkwell Esplanade, south of Crowstone Avenue, Westcliff-on-Sea, SS0 8HU | Getting there Between Chalkwell and Westcliff stations | Hours Accessible 24 hours | Tip On the front, off Palmeira Avenue, is a wonderful stretch of fish and chip restaurants. Local wags claim that there is just one huge subterranean kitchen serving the entire run of outlets.

89 Surviving Mulberry Harbour

Beware – World War II hardware in the sea

This is not for the faint-hearted, even though it's so tempting. A genuine World War II military artefact, a Mulberry Harbour no less, is now wrecked on a sandbank stuck out in the water just over a mile from Thorpe Bay Yacht Club. Only attempt a visit if your name is Mark Spitz.

Mulberry harbours were floating artificial structures built to protect and supply ships anchored off the Normandy coast after the D-Day landings of June 6, 1944. They were to be used until major French ports could be captured and brought back into use after being sabotaged by the Nazis. Mulberries weren't tested here but at Wigtown Bay in the Solway Firth where the tides were similar to those of Normandy. This one is a 2,500-tonne concrete Phoenix caisson.

Brave folk walk out to it, some for a dare, most only after voraciously researching the tide times, otherwise – you know what. There are two deep channels between the Mulberry and the shore, and they fill up before the water covers the sand. If you're caught out, head north-west but beware shells and sharp stones, oh and the added danger of explosives.

Southend's coastguards have now issued warnings, for people have been cut off, surprised that the water between land and the harbour moves about a bit. The coastguards have spoken about a lack of awareness about the natural rhythm of tides. They explain that the tide is usually low enough to walk out for about four and a half hours after high water, which gives the explorer around 45 minutes at the Mulberry. Also, that an average walker will take 45 minutes each way.

Just to add to the problems, the Americans, who won the war for Britain, now believe that the vast resources used on Mulberries may have been wasted, as their forces didn't need them. Well. Too late.

Address In the sea! south of Thorpe Esplanade | Hours Accessible at low tide – but do take care | Tip Head back to dry land on Thorpe Esplanade for a safe seaside stroll, admiring the gaily coloured beach huts and the contemplation of a seriously good quality ice cream at Rossi's.

90__ Three Clocks o'Clock

Maybe better to ask a policeman

You're in a hurry. You're desperate to know the time, having forgotten your phone, watch and sundial. You look up at the bizarre new University of Essex accommodation blocks and there are three damned clocks! Yes, why have one clock when you can have three, and what is the time anyway right at that moment? The furthest dial to the left shows the hour, the middle one shows the minute, and the one on the right the second. The clocks only work if they're looked at together. But by the time you've worked it out it's time to put the clocks back for the autumn. Locals were soon confused, and so were students who can't tell the time with old-fashioned dial clocks as opposed to digital numerical displays.

If you think that's bad, what about these accommodation blocks that house more than five hundred students? They're big, they're brash, they're bold. They sport a headache-inducing array of in-yer-face colours, and were immediately denounced by one local as looking like 'a child's toy, like Lego'. Yet Southend council's member for planning and transport, Anna Waite, soon went public, defending the building and the fancy clocks. This was after there had been a huge local row about spending £5,000 moving the Millennium Clock at the top of the High Street.

More bad news. A national student poll named the accommodation as the ugliest university building in the country, the organisers of the vote noting how 'nestled among what appears to be a quite normal looking suburban area, the multi-coloured monstrosity rises into the sky, blinding students with its bright, day-glo colours. No one wants to live there'.

What else could go wrong? After the university emphasised how they had created 'iconic (sic) buildings which deliver exceptional facilities', it was discovered that the colourful controversial chunks are crammed with contentious cladding! It's all got to go.

Address 36 Queens Road, Southend-on-Sea, SS1 1BF | **Getting there** The hideous blocks are halfway between Southend Victoria and Southend Central stations | **Hours** Viewable from the outside only | **Tip** Head a mile north to ancient Prittlewell Priory and muse over the fact that little-known Prittlewell is the oldest settlement here, Southend being so named because it was the south end of Prittlewell.

91 __ Town to City – at last!
It took a tragedy

David Amess, one of the most popular MPs in the country, had long campaigned for city status for his beloved Southend, one of Britain's most enjoyable seaside resorts. Amess was a working-class Tory and MP for Southend West. He was a devout Catholic who opposed abortion and supported capital punishment. He never held major office, preferring local work.

On Friday 15 October, 2021, Amess was brutally slain at his surgery at Belfairs Methodist Church Hall in nearby Leigh-on-Sea. Inside the church hall, Ali Harbi Ali, later described in court as a 'committed fanatical radicalised Islamist terrorist', had emerged from a group of constituents and fatally stabbed Amess multiple times. His murder was only the sixth targeted homicide of a British MP in a hundred years. The previous such killing was that of Jo Cox in Yorkshire in 2016, following which Amess wrote in his autobiography that fears of such attacks 'spoil the great British tradition of the people openly meeting their elected politicians'.

Amess had hoped to win Southend the new city award as part of the Queen's Platinum Jubilee celebrations of 2022, but instead it took this tragedy for Southend to become a city at last. Three days after his murder, on 18 October, 2021, the Prime Minister announced in Parliament that the Queen had 'provisionally accorded city status to one of the applicants, Southend-on-Sea', which saw Prince Charles present letters patent to the council on 1 March, 2022.

That such a terrible incident could happen here shocked people. Leigh-on-Sea and Southend have long enjoyed a reputation as pleasant, quiet, calm, carefree seaside havens, magnets for daytrippers, enjoying the seven miles of coastline, the warm, soft sands, the ozone, the world's longest pleasure pier, the arcades, amusement park and its ambience as one of the warmest and driest parts of the country.

Address Southend-on-Sea, SS1 2JY (town centre) | **Getting there** Train from London from either Liverpool Street or Fenchurch Street; by car, both the A127 and the A13 connect with the M25 | **Hours** Accessible 24 hours | **Tip** The centre of Southend has been spoilt by the usual urban blight, concrete brutalism, pointless one-way systems and ugly pedestrianisation, but south, away from the central zones, is one of Britain's greatest seaside resorts.

92 World's Longest Pier
Peerless

You can almost get to Kent, or maybe France, so parents convince gullible children when they set foot on Southend Pier, the world's longest at around one-and-a-third miles. It is also halfway along one of Britain's greatest coastal walks, which starts near Shoeburyness, through Thorpe Bay, central Southend, Westcliff and Chalkwell, and finishes past Old Leigh when having reached the creeks that demand turning back, folk wish they'd given up half a mile before for a pint in the Peterboat, Crooked Billet or Olde Smack.

Southend grew in the 19th century as Londoners crammed in the capital came seeking sun, sand and servings of whelks doused in vinegar to foil the taste of the salty sea. Because the coast here consists of large mudflats, the sea is never very deep, even at full tide, large boats are unable to stop near the beach, and so the townsfolk built a pier. Now the boats could get to Southend.

The foundation stone was laid on 25 July, 1829 and the pier was later extended and extended, rebuilt and rebuilt, and by 1848 was the longest in Europe. The pier soon sported its own railway. After World War II visitor numbers shot up to more than five million a year, attracted to amenities such as the Dolphin Café, Sun Deck Theatre, the Solarium Café, the Hall of Mirrors and the obligatory fruit machines. Surprise, surprise a fire erupted – in 1959 – indeed piers keep getting caught in fires. Five hundred people had to be rescued by boat.

In the 1960s, holiday makers began to seek thrills abroad and the pier slowly declined. Another fire badly damaged the structure in 1976, the railway was later deemed unsafe, and closed. But this century there has been considerable investment and now the pier stands proudly to emphasise Southend's status as one of the great seaside resorts. As the eminent poet John Betjeman once said: 'The Pier is Southend, Southend is the Pier.'

Address Off Western Esplanade, Southend-on-Sea, SS 1 2EH, +44 (0)1702 212534, www.southendpier.co.uk | Getting there Train to Southend Central or Southend Victoria | Hours Mon–Fri 10.15am–6pm, Sat & Sun 10.15am–8pm | Tip No visit to Southend is complete without a visit to Adventure Island to bring out your inner 8-year-old.

93 Ancient Aerodrome
We have clearance, Clarence

Stow Maries is so old in the history of aviation, it was used in the Great War by 37 Squadron of the Royal Flying Corps, not the RAF, which didn't then exist. The Air Ministry had categorised the site as an aerodrome as it did not have paved runways, but was just a grassed field that allowed aircraft to take off and land no matter which way the wind was blowing. Nevertheless, the aerodrome is one of the oldest surviving in the world, as well as the best-preserved airfield with Great War era buildings.

The site was first surveyed in August 1916, but Stow Maries was not able to take aircraft until May 1917 when more than 200 personnel arrived. At that stage the government was worried about German Zeppelins and Gotha Bombers, and Stow Maries played a vital role in protecting the east of England in what became known as the First Battle of Britain. It was all part of a plan to create airfields across the east, from Dover to Edinburgh, each to be sited between 10 and 30 miles from each other.

Stow Maries was beset by tragedy. In April 1918, Lieutenant Cyril Milburn's Sopwith Camel aircraft went through a gap in the hedge after it stalled on take-off and exploded in a fireball, killing Milburn. Although Sopwith Camels were equipped with Vickers machine guns that were mounted directly in front of the pilot and would fire at what was directly before them, they were known to be unreliable: of the 10 pilots using the camels at Stow Maries, eight died in accidents while two were shot down by the Royal Navy.

After the war, Stow Maries was handed to the new Royal Air Force. It wasn't used during World War II, and the site went back to agriculture, yet many of the original buildings have survived. In 2009, enthusiasts were successful in reviving it as a light aerodrome given it is Europe's only remaining unaltered World War I Aerodrome. There's also a museum.

Address Hackmans Lane, Flambird's Chase, Chelmsford, CM3 6RJ, +44 (0)1245 429134, www.stowmaries.org.uk | Getting there Stow Maries is about half way between Maldon and South Woodham Ferrers, and is two miles north-east of the latter station | Hours Fri–Sun 10am–4pm | Tip Nearby Maldon, six miles north, features a host of historic buildings, including the 15th-century Moot Hall, where members of the powerful local manor met, and which features a unique brick spiral staircase, a Georgian court room, prison and Victorian council chamber.

94 The Cathedral of Essex

For St John the Baptist, St Mary and St Laurence

In Thaxted, stands the county's most beautiful and awe-inspiring church, St John the Baptist with Our Lady and St Laurence, its spire dominating the landscape as the Cathedral of Essex, no less.

The great poet laureate John Betjeman called it 'a joyful and uplifting church', and it lies in the heart of glorious rural north Essex, light years away from the jellied eels of Southend or the concrete wastes of Basildon. Here, the soft landscape and rolling hills inspired the renowned artist Constable, and the locale is dotted with delightful villages sporting names such as Steeple Bumpstead, Wimbish and Radwinter End.

Simon Jenkins in his book *Country Churches* described Thaxted as 'the Queen of Essex. The steeple stands out over the surrounding fields, and the town streets bend in its direction over ancient cobbles and past timber framed houses'. Building began in 1340 and finished in 1510, its magnificence showing off the prosperity that came from the local medieval cutlery and wool trades. In the 15th century, Thaxted took part in the new proto-Protestant cause of Lollardy, and a 'prest of Thaksted' was burnt at London's Smithfield, but the main controversy occurred in the 1920s. The vicar, Conrad le Despenser Roden Noel, a Christian socialist, shocked congregants by hoisting the Red Flag and the Tricolour of Sinn Fein alongside the Union Jack. He also dedicated a room above the north porch to John Ball, a leader of the Peasants' Revolt. Students from Cambridge University staged attacks to remove the flags and the church authorities ordered their removal.

If that wasn't shocking enough, in 1976 vicar Peter Elers declared his homosexuality as one of the first openly gay vicars in the CofE and blessed a lesbian marriage, explaining that if the church could bless battleships and budgerigars, 'it ought to find it in its heart to bless men and women in love'.

Address Watling Street, Thaxted, CM6 2QY, +44 (0)1371 831409, www.ttsrh.org/thaxted |
Getting there The spire dominates the sky in what is a village just south of the junction of
the B 184 and the B 1051 | Hours Daily 10am–6pm | Tip Head south to see John Webb's
magnificent restored windmill, a postcard classic.

95__Thaxted Guildhall
Medieval masterpiece and Morris Men

It looks like John of Gaunt might emerge any moment from this medieval masterwork in limed oak and announce that the king has died, but the Thaxted Guildhall is simply the centrepiece of the splendidly traditional town of Thaxted. The Guildhall was built between 1462 and 1475 as a market and meeting place by the Guild of Cutlers, with an open arcade on the ground floor. Here skilled tradesmen could now regulate their trading practices. Thaxted Grammar School later used the building and it is now a small museum. The building was used by Pevsner on the cover of his 1954 *Buildings of Essex* bible.

Local wealth came from the wool trade as well as cutlery. But after these declined, Thaxted became an agricultural backwater. It was saved commercially in 1870 when George Lee opened both a sweet factory and a light railway, the latter promoted by the gin magnate Sir Walter Gilbey as 'the Gin and Toffee Line'.

Thaxted retains an ancient air, with Georgian Victorian cottages crammed together and a welcome absence of the usual high street chains. There are plenty of pubs, a glorious windmill, and the magnificent church of St John the Baptist (see ch. 94). The sleepy rural bliss is often interrupted in the summer by the arrival of Morris dancers, the Thaxted Morris Ring, in their striped waistcoats and straw hats, waving their handkerchiefs and bashing their broomsticks, headed for Thaxted for a pub crawl before their finale in the High Street.

The early 20th-century composer Gustav Holst fell in love with Thaxted in 1913, and it was in a cottage here, later destroyed by a fire, that he worked on *The Planets*. Holst had been declared unfit for military service, and during the Great War was regarded with suspicion on account of his Germanic name. He later renamed his universally loved hymn 'I Vow To Thee My Country' from *The Planets Suite*'s 'Jupiter' as 'Thaxted'.

Address Town Street, Thaxted, Dunmow, CM6 2LA, +44 (0)1371 830856, www.facebook.com/guildhallthaxted | **Getting there** The Guildhall is half way between the parish church and the B 1051 | **Hours** Easter to end Sept Sun & Bank Holidays 2–6pm | **Tip** Head to Horham Hall, a Grade I 16th-century mansion south-east of the town. When Queen Elizabeth stayed here in 1571 she was most upset to discover that there was a plot to place Mary, Queen of Scots on her throne.

96 Grave of Jack the Ripper?

The sceptre shan't depart from Judah until Shiloh

It's still the biggest crime mystery of the last two hundred years. Who was Jack the Ripper? Despite the never-ending books, TV programmes, experts and theories about who killed the five women in London's East End in 1888, informed analysis keeps on going back to Sir William Gull, Physician in Ordinary to Queen Victoria, who is buried here in St Michael churchyard in the remote village of Thorpe-le-Soken.

The claim that Gull was not just the Ripper but one of a team came in the 1950s from an elderly artist, Joseph Sickert, son of the better-known Walter, so he claimed, who explained that a team including Gull, acting on behalf of Prince Eddy, Queen Victoria's errant grandson, killed the women. This was to prevent their black-mailing the prince over his illegal marriage to a Catholic shop girl, Annie Crook, in a chapel in Wellclose Square, east London. Gull may even have killed them to prevent one of the women giving birth to an illegitimate royal child. Detractors on Wikipedia claim 'a widely discredited Masonic royal conspiracy theory [alleges] that Gull knew Jack the Ripper or even that he himself was the murderer', when the only discrediting has come from Freemasons covering up the story.

Ripper or not, William Gull died in 1890 and was buried near his Colchester birthplace. His gravestone does not reveal his religious affiliation, but Gull was a follower of the early 19th-century false prophet Joanna Southcott, who had claimed she would give birth to Shiloh, saviour of mankind, as predicted in the Old Testament. In the most extreme Ripper theory yet, Gull aborted the foetuses because he was convinced that one of the women, having been with the future king, could give birth to the false Shiloh that might destroy the royal family.

So that's settled that then. The gravestone has been vandalised, probably by followers of a different theory.

Address High Street, Thorpe-le-Soken, Clacton-on-Sea, CO16 0ED | Getting there The church is by the junction of the B 1033 and B 1414 | Hours Open during daylight hours | Tip Have a stroll along to Comarques, an 18th-century mansion where the revered early 20th-century author Arnold Bennett lived, and possibly Clement Attlee as a child.

97 __ Amazon's Depot
Deliver yourself to their door

For centuries, Amazon was simply a mighty river. Now it's the world's best-known delivery company, and here in Tilbury, by one of the world's greatest docks, is a massive depot, a Fulfilment Centre no less, bigger than 28 football stadiums.

Amazon now allows the public to visit these centres to see how it holds tens of millions of items a day. Here, 'world class tour leaders' (how can that be verified?) show you around and explain how packages make their journey from the click of the button on the laptop to the knock on the door from a courier asking the owner: 'Are you Mr Josiah Foodbotham of No. 10 Acacia Grove, Utley, Yorkshire?' only to be told, 'No. I'm Mrs Josie Foodbotham of No. 10 Acacia Grove, Ugley, Essex', or something like that.

Amazon was founded by Jeff Bezos in 1994 in Seattle, the city chosen for its abundance of technical talent. If you've ever wondered how that product in your online shopping cart gets from Amazon to you, you can now see for yourself. Within this mighty cavernous space, under a comfortable skylit climate kept at room temperature year round, fork lift truck drivers tussle with robots to get the items on balancing towers in what they say looks like a choreographed dance across shiny concrete floors as shipping labels fly onto boxes blown by puffs of air.

The Amazon robots are really smart, and place items into a yellow plastic box called a tote while Amnesty Floor Monitors – humans – make sure the floors are clear. Surprisingly, instead of items being stored like in a shop, electronics on one aisle, books on another, say, all the goods at the fulfilment centres are stowed randomly. Yellow tiered pods stack bins full of unrelated items, all of which are tracked by computers. It works.

There are 175 of these worldwide. Tilbury, with its docks, is ideal for the new mega container ships and this plant has created 1,500 jobs.

Address London Distribution Park, Windrush Road, Tilbury, RM18 7AN, +44 (0)7482 247503, www.amazon.jobs/en-gb/locations/tilbury-uk | Getting there The centre is just east off the A 1089, half a mile north of the Thames; train to Grays, which is half a mile to the west, or Tilbury Town | Hours Regularly change, so visit the website for information | Tip Head to the bizarre upside-down house by Chafford Hundred station, where you can walk across the ceiling. Ideal for budding astronauts.

98__Bata-Ville Shoe City
The sole of Tilbury

Essex – the land of the model village and utopian schemes. One of the most successful has been Bata-Ville in Tilbury, built for the Czech company Bata, 'Quality Shoes and Bags for Women, Men and Kids Since 1894'.

Bata was founded by Tomáš Baťa who went to America to see Henry Ford's conveyor belt system, and copied it to become one of the world's biggest multinational retailers and distributors of what the retail trade call footwear (shoes to normal people). In the spirit of idealism common among progressives between the wars, Baťa wanted the best for his workers. His model village in his home town of Zlín was based on Letchworth in Hertfordshire, and he copied it here for 3,000 workers, hiring the Czech architects Frantizek Gahura and Vladimir Karfik. Karfik even worked with Le Corbusier who visited Zlín and was full of praise. 'I perceived a much more valued and effective factor – the human heart.'

Gahura and Karfik's houses are cuboid, cosy and spacious. Bata-ville had schools, sports facilities, cinema and a fire station. Residents bought milk in the Bata supermarket and eggs at the company farm. They had to keep their gardens tidy or a Bata agent would call them to the office and order them to be a bit more Percy Thrower-ish with the delphiniums, lest they might not triumph at the annual summer gardening competition. There was an annual pre-season football match between Bata and West Ham, with the inevitably losing West Ham team each given a free pair of shoes.

After Baťa died in a plane accident in 1932, his brother, Jan, carried on. But under communism in post-war Czechoslovakia the company was nationalised and declined here. By the end of the century, there were only 200 employees left in Tilbury. The factory closed in 2005, moving manufacturing to Malaysia. The listed factory buildings are now owned by a storage company, and the estate is rundown.

Address Bata Factory and Estate, Princess Avenue, East Tilbury, RM18 8ST; Radical Essex produce a useful leaflet outlining a Bata Estate Walking Tour, www.radicalessex.uk/wp-content/uploads/2017/06/Bata-Estate-Walking-Tour.pdf | **Getting there** Train to East Tilbury; by car, follow Princess Margaret Road | **Hours** Visit www.bataheritagecentre.org.uk for details of Open Days | **Tip** The main exhibition displays relating to the factory and estate can be viewed in the East Tilbury Library, Princess Avenue, RM18 8ST.

99 *Empire Windrush* Landing Point

This is my country

It's the most famous immigrant ship in British history. On 22 June, 1948 the *Empire Windrush* arrived from Kingston, Jamaica, at Tilbury Docks bringing 1,027 Caribbean citizens and two stowaways to Britain in search of a new life – rain, wind and Spam instead of sun, sea and yam. It was also carrying 66 people registered as Mexican who were really Polish, having travelled from Siberia via India and the Pacific.

The ship was the German-owned *Monte Rosa*, used by the Nazis to spread their ideology to South America. But now ads were placed in West Indian newspapers offering cheap transport – £28 – for anyone who wanted to come and work in the UK, mostly as public transport workers or staff for the new NHS. Some passengers were put into deep subterranean shelters built for protection against atomic bombs in Clapham South tube station.

The arrivals included Sam Beaver King, who went on to co-found the Notting Hill Carnival and become the first black mayor of Southwark; Nancy Cunard, not exactly an immigrant, heiress to the Cunard shipping fortune, on her way back from Trinidad; and most excitingly of all the calypso musician Lord Beginner who wrote the legendary song 'Victory Test Match' about the West Indies' 1950 first ever test cricket win in London, which contained the wonderful lines 'Cricket, Lovely Cricket, at Lord's where I saw it / Yardley tried his best / but Goddard won the Test / With those little pals of mine, Ramadhin and Valentine'. The celebration procession then danced its way from the ground to the Eros statue in Piccadilly Circus.

In 2012, to widespread shock, the Tory-Liberal Coalition government forced the now decades older Windrush generation to prove they had the right to stay in Britain, even though they had arrived as children on their parents' passports.

Address Southernmost point of the A 1089 by the Thames | Getting there Train to Tilbury Town | Hours Accessible 24 hours | Tip Have a look at the Norman church of St James, outside which Queen Elizabeth spoke before the Spanish Armada, and around which the area revolved until 1979 when it was closed. It is now private apartments.

100___ Tilbury Docks
'By Thames to All People of the World'

London's main port isn't in London. It's 25 miles east of London Bridge here in Tilbury by a loop in the Thames. There used to be a series of docks in the capital itself that stretched over miles east of London Bridge, but they all closed in the late 20th century, whereas Tilbury marches on.

Tilbury Docks were built in the 1880s on a marshy soil of unexpected blue clay. The docks brought work that was not only arduous but appallingly paid and so the dockers were happy to join the 1889 strike for 'the dockers' tanner' – to be paid sixpence an hour. In 1903, Tilbury became an important place for passengers, as well as goods when P&O arrived. Thirty years later, a new cruise terminal was built. But the most significant development came in 1965 when the new roll-on roll-off system was adopted. Previously, the men had carried goods such as chests of tea off the ship all day. Inevitably, a chest or two would break open as the dockers became more tired and the loose tea would lie there for the rest of the day, the men walking on it, having been to the open-air toilets. At the end of the day they would scoop up the loose contaminated tea, pack it in an empty chest, and send it off. That is why everyone died at the age of 40.

Now, roll-on roll-off meant huge ships packed with massive containers that literally did roll off. No old-fashioned dockers were needed, the tea came vacuum packed, and nobody got sick. Inevitably the changes meant more strikes, but the dockers did themselves no favours by marching in support of Enoch Powell's racist 'Rivers of Blood' speech in 1968. They carried placards reading 'Back Britain, not Black Britain', which was most ironic given that it was at Tilbury that the first West Indian immigrants arrived in Britain in 1948 on the *Empire Windrush* ship (see ch. 99) and that foreigners had been arriving in Britain here for centuries.

Address Tilbury, RM18 7EH | Getting there Train to Tilbury Town; by car, A 1089 by the Thames | Hours Viewable from a distance, or contact +44 (0)1787 226995 to reserve a place on a site visit | Tip Take a ferry across the Thames to Gravesend bathed in maritime history and its Dickens connections.

101 Tilbury Fort

Redoubtable repellent

Look at a map of south Essex and Tilbury. You can see why the latter town had to be formidably defended over the centuries. Fittingly, Tilbury Fort is one of Britain's greatest citadels, with moats and bastioned outworks, right by the Thames estuary, and it protected the seaward approach to London from the 16th century to World War II.

Henry VIII built the first fort in Tilbury in 1539, building repellents along the English coastline and giving instructions for 'the defence of the realm in time of invasion'. It came into its own when Queen Elizabeth I rallied her troops here before facing the Armada with her famous speech: 'I know I have the body of a weak and feeble woman; but I have the heart and stomach of a king.'

After Dutch naval raids during the 17th century, the fort was enlarged to form a star-shaped defence, with two lines of guns facing the river, believed to be the best in Britain. Scottish prisoners were held here following Bonnie Prince Charlie's unsuccessful Jacobite rebellion of 1745, and more and more artillery batteries were added over the years, in particular to protect against raiders and invaders aiming for the Woolwich Arsenal and the victualling yards of Deptford.

As military technology advanced in the 19th century, Tilbury became less important as a fighting force and was used merely to move troops and store ammo, being decommissioned in 1950. Tilbury Fort is now an English Heritage tourist attraction. It was also put to excellent use in 2018 by the film director Mike Leigh who used it to shoot the formidable scenes of the troops attacking the ordinary people of Manchester in 1819 for his Peterloo Massacre picture. Although it is believed no one has ever died at Tilbury, a local legend has it that at a game of cricket here in 1776 one team was accused of fielding a professional player, a row broke out, and a man was shot dead.

Address Tilbury, RM18 7NR, +44 (0)370 3331181, www.english-heritage.org.uk/visit/ places/tibury-fort | **Getting there** Half a mile east of Tilbury off the A 126; train to Tilbury Town, then a short walk | **Hours** Fri–Sun 10am–5pm | **Tip** Two miles east is Tilbury Fort's brother, the Coalhouse Fort.

102— Wells Coates Sunspan Home
Pick it up and take it away with you

Essex was one of THE places in England during the 20th century for experimental progressive modernist houses. They're everywhere – in Canvey, Frinton (see ch. 40) and here in the Chadwell St Mary corner of north Tilbury. This wonder of stone and solarity was designed by the Canadian Wells Wintemute Coates (1895 – 1958) whose best-known work is the socially advanced 1930s block Isokon in Hampstead.

Sunspan House captures the inspiration of the 20th-century's greatest architect and town planner, Le Corbusier, and his mantra, 'a house is a machine for living in', highlighting the future in gleaming white and splashes of sun. The Sunspan houses were the first ever pre-fabricated houses. They were designed around a square standing at an angle to the road so that they were south facing, allowing light into two sides of the building. This was their main aim: allow the maximum amount of sun into the house, an ideal of the new architects and social dreamers of the 1930s. Then war came and ruined everything.

Here, Coates worked with David Pleydell-Bouverie to create an entry for the Ideal Home Exhibition of 1934 as an example of what housing could be. Wells Coates' best-known idea was to create houses that were so adaptable they could be packed up, put on a truck, and taken on holiday. No, not a caravan! Ingenious internal planning meant that rooms could be reshaped at a whim. The fireplace is a riot of beautiful brick, the cupboards have sliding wood doors, the curved staircase is decorated with chrome, and the bathroom has an apse. The system worked for all sorts of varieties: one bedroom and five bedrooms. Sunspan houses were also built in Southsea, Welwyn and Inverness. This one sits in greenbelt land with captivating views towards the Thames; the garden has a World War II air raid shelter. It recently went on sale for £475,000 after being empty and neglected for years.

Address Sandy Lane, Chadwell St Mary, Thurrock, RM16 4LR | Getting there By car, take the B149 to Chadwell St Mary | Hours Viewable from the outside only | Tip Time for liquid refreshment. Head to the ancient white weatherboarded riverside World's End pub on Fort Road.

103 — Layer Marney Tower

Tallest Tudor turrets

Essex is verily the land of weird follies, eccentric towers and bizarre constructions, and here is Layer Marney Tower, the tallest Tudor Gatehouse in the country, looking mightily incongruous in between cosy houses in delightful countryside. There are 99 steps to the top of what looks like eight floors but are simply double windows confusingly built to make the tower look higher and more packed than it is.

Layer Marney is built of red brick, the colour chosen to stand out, mixed with black glazed bricks for diapering decoration. It was built in the 1520s by Henry, First Lord Marney, Henry VIII's Captain of the Bodyguard and Lord Privy Seal, as an egotistical statement in an era of one-upmanship inspired by a king who believed a building should reflect the magnificence of its owner. Around the tower there was supposed to be a palace, but it was never finished, for Marney died in 1523 and his son two years later. As there were no male heirs to continue the family line, all that was built was the main range 300 feet long, some outbuildings, a new church and this, the principal gatehouse. Nevertheless, what stands provides a glimpse into the grand aspirations of a 16th-century lord.

The buildings suffered in 1884 from that English rarity, an earthquake. *The Builder* magazine explained that the outlay needed to restore the tower to 'anything like a sound and habitable condition would be so large the chance of the work ever being done appears remote indeed'. They were wrong. It was well restored and in its imminent Edwardian heyday it was serviced by 13 domestic and 16 external staff. Wedding receptions and conferences now take place in the tower, and film companies have been here for *Lovejoy* and the *Antiques Roadshow*. Layer Marney is still a family home and no, the occupants do not walk around dressed in suits of armour fulminating against the Reformation.

Address East Court, off Roundbush Road, Layer Marney, CO5 9US, +44 (0)1206 330784, www.layermarneytower.co.uk | **Getting there** Layer Marney Tower is midway between Colchester and Tiptree, just off the B 1022; train to Smythe's Green | **Hours** 1 May – 13 July Sun & Wed, 17 July – 1 Sept Sun – Thu, 4 – 25 Sept Sun & Wed 11am – 5pm | **Tip** Nearby Hedingham Castle has the best Norman keep in England.

104__ Tiptree Jam Museum
Jam today – and tomorrow

Tiptree is home to Jobserve, the world's first online recruitment service, but this is fruitier. This is one of the sweetest small museums in the country, based inside a barn at the factory where the renowned Tiptree brand is produced. Highlights include a four-legged chicken, a map of the route of the local Crab and Winkle Railway, which included a stop at Tiptree, an ancient clocking-in machine and the world's first automatic jam jar filler (a 1950s contraption that could fill 60 jars per minute) alongside random objects, information boards and the story of the brand. No wonder according to a hoary legend the French revolutionaries had a well-known saying: 'Liberty, equality, Tiptree jam!'

Originally, Tiptree was the Britannia Fruit Preserving Company. John Wilkin, the owner, was inspired by an 1883 William Gladstone speech, and he even sent the great prime minister a jar from the first batch, receiving back in turn a handwritten note thanking him for the 'agreeable present'. The family name Wilkin still appears on some jars today but it was later renamed Tiptree after its location.

During the Great War, Wilkin & Sons sent 8,000 boxes of jam to the Front, while in World War II during rationing, Tiptree launched a temporary brand, Unitree, to avoid tarnishing their name with what might be considered lower quality goods. Artefacts for the museum were fortuitously saved from the scrapheap by chance in the 1970s when the company founder's grandson had the foresight to save discarded objects, and the collection first opened to the public in the 1990s.

After all that jamming, it's time for tea, with a scone, naturally, and you know what on it. The shop sells all manner of Tiptree products, not just jams but sauces, spirits, sweets and other gifts. And if you're really lucky you might be able to do a good turn for the day by helping a damson in distress.

Address Factory Hill, Tiptree, CO5 0RF, +44 (0)1621 814524, www.tiptree.com | Getting there Just off the B 1023; by train to Kelvedon or Witham, then a three-mile walk | Hours Mon–Sat 9.30am–5pm, Sun 10am–5pm but hours subject to change, so telephone first | Tip Make a visit to the strikingly garish pink expanse of the nearby Pink House, artist Amy Griffith's six-bedroom mansion, which has been used for music video shoots and attracted sleb visitors such as the equally *outré* concoction Paris Hilton. Also available on Airbnb so you can experience it for yourself.

105 — Remains of the Old Abbey

Bring in the body

This ancient religious stronghold was one of the great medieval monasteries. It is also one of the most important historical sites in the immediate environs north of London. There has been a church on the site since the seventh century, but only traces of flint rubble under the present choir remain. Major drama occurred in the 11th century when one Tovi the Proud, an Anglo-Danish chieftain, loaded a black crucifix found at Montacute in Somerset onto an ox-cart without a care in the world only to find the ox refusing to go any way but the road to Waltham, a journey of 150 miles. Worshippers explained that this clearly meant the cross was holy. They also claimed it had healing powers. The holy cross was placed inside the church and saw many arrive on pilgrimages, including Harold Godwin, Earl of Wessex, who was miraculously cured of paralysis praying before it.

Harold's son, the eventual King Harold II, refounded the church, and stopped to pray here on his way to fight William of Normandy at the Battle of Stamford Bridge (brief pause not to make any Chelsea jokes). At the later Battle of Hastings, the warrior cry of the English troops was 'Holy Cross', but Hastings was disastrous and saw the end of Harold, who it is believed was buried here. But was it really Harold's body? His concubine, Edith Swanneck, recognised it only through what she said were secret marks. The body, royal or not, has been moved several times and is now thought to be to the west of two marker stones, one of which bears the inscription *This stone marks the position of the high altar behind which King Harold is said to have been buried in 1066*, and the other *Harold King of England OBVT 1066*.

The later Augustinian abbey became the last in England to be dissolved when it fell in 1540. Now little remains on what is still a fascinating site to explore.

Address Abbey View, Waltham Abbey, EN9 1XQ | Getting there Train to Waltham Cross, then a 25-minute walk or short bus ride; by car, take the A 121 then B 194 | Hours Accessible 24 hours | Tip Explore the nearby River Lea where there are so many tributaries, backwaters and reservoirs the map-makers can barely cope.

106__Ring Out Wild Bells
In Memoriam

The bells of the Abbey Church of Waltham Holy Cross and St Lawrence are no ordinary bells. They inspired one of the best-known poems in the English language – 'In Memoriam' by Alfred, Lord Tennyson, in particular the section 'Ring Out, Wild Bells', published in 1850, the year he was appointed Poet Laureate:

Ring out, wild bells, to the wild sky/The flying cloud, the frosty light:/The year is dying in the night.

The poem is Tennyson's elegy to his best pal, Arthur Hallam, who died of a ruptured aneurysm at the age of 22. The two had formed a deep friendship at Cambridge, and it grew when Hallam became engaged to Alfred's sister Emily. The two men travelled abroad where Tennyson was inspired to write one of his most famous works, 'The Lady of Shalott'. When Hallam died, Tennyson was bereft of a soulmate. He began to write a number of elegies for Hallam and these were eventually connected as 'In Memoriam'.

Tennyson was staying nearby at High Beach when he heard the bells being rung on New Year's Eve. That night was particularly stormy and the wind, rather than the ringers, was doing the swinging. The story is honoured at Manchester Town Hall where the hour bell, Great Abel, has the lines *Ring out the false, ring in the true* cast upon it.

Tennyson became the most revered poet of the Victorian era, honoured by the Queen with a peerage and top appointment, his 'Locksley Hall' (1842) the pinnacle:

Comrades, leave me here a little, while as yet 'tis early morn:/Leave me here, and when you want me, sound upon the bugle-horn./'Tis the place, and all around it, as of old, the curlews call,/Dreary gleams about the moorland flying over Locksley Hall.

In 1974, Tennyson's verses were desecrated by George Harrison for his single 'Ding Dong Ding Dong' with its refrain 'Ring out the old/Ring in the new/Ring out the false, ring in the true'.

Address Church Street, Waltham Abbey, EN9 1DX, +44 (0)1992 767897 | Getting there Train to Waltham Cross, then a 25-minute walk or short bus ride; by car, take the A 121 then B 194 | Hours The bells can be heard constantly, especially every hour; church open Wed & Fri–Sun 10am–4pm but times can change so check with the church before visiting | Tip In the middle of nearby Waltham Cross village is an authentic Eleanor Cross. It is one of only three that have survived of the original 12 that Edward I built in the 1290s in honour of his wife, Eleanor of Castile.

107 Royal Gunpowder Mills
A most explosive entity

Short of ammo? Come to Waltham Abbey's Royal Gunpowder Mills, one of the most important sites not just in the country but in the world for developing explosives. The site is right by the River Lea and its innumerable tributaries, channels and waterways – perfect for power and transport, taking the goods to the great magazines at Purfleet and Woolwich for the navy and army.

Bangs, booms and blasts have been designed here since 1665, even though two people were killed by a powder mill as soon as it opened. As the British Empire grew so did this site, and in 1787 the Crown replaced the Walton family as owners, making all private manufacturers produce gunpowder to this standard. By the end of the 19th century, the era of gunpowder was drawing to a close and new forces such as cordite came into play. Out went the old steam engines and in came electric motors to drive the belts for the mixing machines.

Work was busiest during the two world wars. From 1914–18 more than 6,000 people were employed here, the plant active 24 hours a day, seven days a week. During World War II, Waltham made RDX – Research Department Explosive – a white solid without smell or taste used for the infamous bouncing bomb during the Dambusters raid, which was tested in a nearby woodland pond.

By its very nature the site has witnessed accidents, incidents and fatalities. In January 1940 there were two massive explosions in the woodlands due to over-zealous involvement with nitro-glycerine. The explosions blew windows as far away as the East End and were registered at Kew Gardens. Not only did five men die, three were never discovered – they just exploded into thin air.

Production ceased here in 1943 and the site became an MOD research establishment until the 1990s when it was turned into a visitor attraction, and the woodland designated as a Site of Special Scientific Interest.

Address Beaulieu Drive, Waltham Abbey, EN9 1JY, +44 (0)1992 707370, www.royalgunpowdermills.com | Getting there Train to Waltham Cross, then a 25-minute walk or short bus ride; by car, take the A 121 then B 194 | Hours Easter–end Oct Sun & Bank Holidays 11am–4.30 pm | Tip Epping Forest District Museum is half a mile southeast at 39–41 Sun Street.

108 Naze Tower
On the naze

It's an ugly coloured gawky mini monstrosity of an elongated octagonal tower over eight floors. Certainly no looker, but the Naze Tower does serve as a focal point for the delightful seaside resort of Walton-on-the-Naze, or what Daniel Defoe called 'Walton, under the Nase', but certainly an improvement on the Saxon Eadolfenaesse.

Naze tower was built in the 1720s by the naval authority Trinity House to aid seamen guiding their vessels through the Goldmer Gap. It had a cousin of a tower at Walton Hall. Thousands of ships used Harwich port each year and the tower would be topped with beacons or lamps that were vital, as the coast is rather featureless. Naze Tower was used in the 18th century as a tea house. It was run by a Martha Ray, an actress who was murdered in Covent Garden. In the Napoleonic Wars and Great War, the tower was the perfect lookout, but in World War II its crenellations were removed so that it could be used as a radar station. Around the tower more than 20,000 tonnes of granite rocks from Norway have been placed at the base of the cliffs to protect them from the sea, but a 500-foot walkway along the top means visitors can now reach the cliffs and the 50-million-year-old fossils.

The tower is now privately owned, refurbished so that it is now no longer likely to fall into the sea. It is open, so you can now go up all 86 feet of its 111 spiral steps for panoramic views across the Naze. There is a museum with exhibits about the tower, the ecology and geology of the Naze, and the problems of coastal erosion, which is slowly eating away the cliffs. Think that's an over-reaction? The medieval village of Walton now lies nine miles out to sea.

Walton, Naze, Nase or Nose, is a friendly family resort with sandy beaches, quaint narrow streets and plenty of opportunities for fossil hunting. Its pier is the second longest in England, beaten only by Southend.

Address Old Hall Lane, Walton-on-the-Naze, CO14 8LE, +44 (0)7966 776417, www.nazetower.co.uk | **Getting there** Train to Walton-on-the-Naze, then a 30-minute walk along the sea front; by car, head north along the B 1035 towards the beach huts | **Hours** Daily 1 Apr – 31 Oct 10am – 5pm | **Tip** It's got to be the Naze itself, located just north of Walton-on-the-Naze, with its cliffs and nature reserve, perfect for walking and bird watching.

109 _ Secret Water
Arthur Ransome's children's classic

A 2022 Essex Book Festival poll found that Arthur Ransome's 1939 *Secret Water*, ostensibly a children's book, but in reality a must for children of all ages, is the greatest ever Essex novel. 1939? Rather than deal with the horrors of Europe about to go to war, Hitler's land-grabbing, and the planned extermination of the Jewish race, it is pure escapism – gentle, heart-warming, life-affirming.

Secret Water is Hamford Water, a marshy expanse halfway between Harwich and Walton-on-the-Naze by the North Sea. It is a tidal inlet with marsh grasslands, creeks, mud, salt marshes, islands and beaches, and now a 5,000-acre biological Site of Special Scientific Interest. Eco groups have described it as being of 'international importance for breeding little terns and wintering Brent geese', among other bird species. There are rare plants such as hog's fennel and slender hare's-ear, one of Britain's scarcest coastal plants.

Secret Water was the eighth book in the *Swallows and Amazons* series in which the heroes are joined by new characters, the Eels and the Mastodon. The story begins only a few days after its equally wonderful predecessor, *We Didn't Mean To Go To Sea*, finishes as the cast head to Hamford Water to camp with their father who is then called away on naval business. Ransome was well acquainted with sailing in the area and set the book here so that his characters had new places to explore and make maps.

The main land mass here is Horsey Island, which is surrounded by creeks and inlets, not just Hamford Water but Walton Channel, Kirby Creek and The Wade. For those of a fishier frame of mind there is the smaller Kipper's Island to the west. Best avoid Bramble Island, as it is used for explosives testing.

There are other problems. According to local novelist Ursula Bloom, 'too much land has slipped into the sea. It's a thieving sea.' Catch it while you can.

Address CO14 | Getting there Train to Kirby Cross; by car, take the Walton Road off the B 1414 | Hours Accessible 24 hours | Tip Get the time of year right, and a trek along the coast with a pair of binoculars might bring you a chance meeting with playful seal pups.

110___The Chapel in the Mall

Shop 'til you drop on your knees

Want a shopping experience with a difference? Head to Lakeside, one of the largest shopping centres in a country filled with them, this one built on the site of a former chalk quarry and opened in 1988 by Princess Alexandra. But if you think a visit to Lakeside is all about emptying the contents of your wallet into various multi-national chains, there is another side to the trip: retail therapy that involves taking on a more spiritual hue. For in the middle of this godless, Mammon-chasing supermall is a chapel for private prayer.

Clearly the Lakeside chapel serves several purposes. Say you've just spent £200 on a jacket as worn by Bethany on *Coronation Street* and are feeling guilty on account of all the suffering in the world. Head to the chapel to seek absolution. Or say you've walked out of a well-known handbag shop and have just noticed that the cashier gave you five pounds too much in change. You quickly spent it on a caramel latte in Starbucks and are now wracked with guilt. Go to the chapel and seek forgiveness.

The chapel is tucked away on the third floor, just off the food court, and so perfect for shoppers who have just scarfed down a bacon sandwich at Greggs and are now torn over Jesus' teachings about the flesh of the pig (*Mark* 7:17–23).

The chapel holds occasional services and has a team of chaplains to provide counselling and spiritual guidance. 'I believe this is the only chapel in a shopping centre, although there are places of quiet,' said former chaplain Colin Phillips. 'It's an oasis of prayer open to all faiths.' More seriously, the clergy have offered their services to workers who have just been made redundant, and on happier days hold carol services, harvest services and even memorial services. But if you have parked your car on Floor 2, Block A, Bay 97 but have lost the piece of paper that tells you so, there's nothing they can do.

Address Level 3, West Thurrock Way, West Thurrock, Grays, RM20 2ZP, +44 (0)1708 450083 | Getting there Lakeside is just south-east of the junction of the A13 and the A282; train to Chafford Hundred | Hours As for the shopping centre: Mon–Sat 9am–9pm, Sun 11am–5pm | Tip What's the one thing you really want to do after you've shopped 'til you dropped? Mess around on the water. Well this is Lakeside, after all, and you can do just that on the Alexandra Lake outside by visiting the Lakeside Diving and Watersports Centre.

111 Church of Gareth's Burial
No weddings but a funeral

It's a heart-rending scene from the highest grossing British film at the time: Gareth's funeral from *Four Weddings and a Funeral*, this being the funeral bit. The film was a smash hit when it burst onto cinema screens in 1994 courtesy of director Mike Newell and scriptwriter Richard Curtis. But then it did parade a galaxy of stars: Hugh Grant (the role that made him), John Hannah, Andie MacDowell, Kristin Scott Thomas, Simon Callow and Rowan Atkinson in a hilarious cameo role as the hapless Catholic priest muddling up the names of the bride and groom.

But it was the on-screen reading by John Hannah of 'Funeral Blues' by W. H. Auden that jerked a thousand tears. John Hannah plays Matthew, distraught at the sudden death of his surprise gay lover Gareth (Simon Callow). Even more surprisingly the scene was shot not in a posh, smart sophisticated London church but this incongruous location, St Clements Church in industrial West Thurrock. Somewhere here there's a joke bursting to get out, for the episode should have been in a soap opera, not a rom-com, as next door to the church is the Procter and Gamble factory, responsible for such luminary toiletries as Head & Shoulders, Pampers, Ariel, Bold and Daz, the latter famous for Danny Baker's doorstep challenge. The locale was chosen precisely because it couldn't have been more out of place.

Procter & Gamble, now an American multi-national, was founded in 1837 by English American William Procter and Irish American James Gamble. It's been part of Essex's industrial landscape for decades, suffusing the atmosphere with its flowery detergenty smells. Regular services stopped in the 1980s because of the winter cold and damp, but Procter & Gamble stepped in to refurbish the church in 1987. If you do get to a service just pray the vicar doesn't get the Holy Ghost and the holy goat mixed up, like Rowan Atkinson.

Address St Clement's Road, Grays, RM20 4AL, +44 (0)1375 377379, www.stclementwthurrock.co.uk | Getting there The church (and soap factory) are a mile east of the Dartford Crossing, right by the Thames. Or just head for Lakeside, then half a mile south; train to Chafford Hundred | Hours 1 Apr–30 Sept first weekend of the month 11am–3pm, and also by arrangement | Tip Explore Grays Chalk Quarry Nature Reserve a mile north-east.

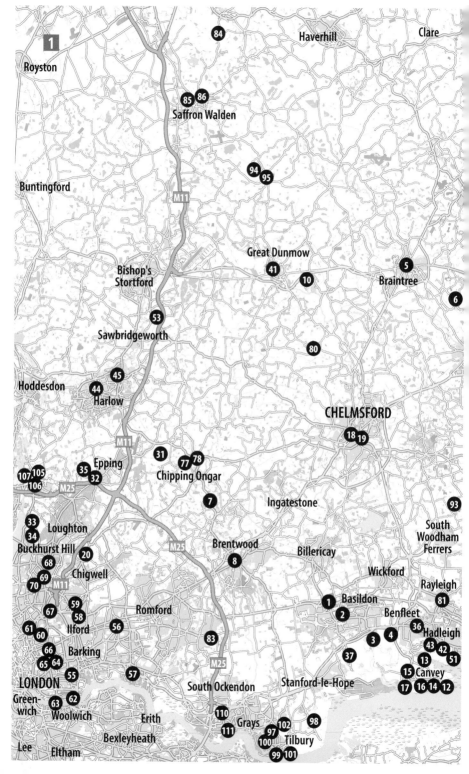

Ed Glinert, David Taylor
**111 Places in Yorkshire
That You Shouldn't Miss**
ISBN 978-3-7408-1167-9

Ed Glinert, Marc Zakian
**111 Places in London's East
End That You Shouldn't Miss**
ISBN 978-3-7408-0752-8

Lindsay Sutton, David Taylor
**111 Places in Lancaster
That You Shouldn't Miss**
ISBN 978-3-7408-1557-8

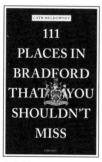

Cath Muldowney
**111 Places in Bradford
That You Shouldn't Miss**
ISBN 978-3-7408-1427-4

Kim Revill, Alesh Compton
**111 Places in Leeds
That You Shouldn't Miss**
ISBN 978-3-7408-0754-2

Michael Glover,
Richard Anderson
**111 Places in Sheffield
That You Shouldn't Miss**
ISBN 978-3-7408-1728-2

Julian Treuherz,
Peter de Figueiredo
**111 Places in Manchester
That You Shouldn't Miss**
ISBN 978-3-7408-0753-5

Julian Treuherz,
Peter de Figueiredo
**111 Places in Liverpool
That You Shouldn't Miss**
ISBN 978-3-7408-1607-0

David Taylor
**111 Places in Newcastle
That You Shouldn't Miss**
ISBN 978-3-7408-1043-6

Katherine Bebo, Oliver Smith
111 Places in Poole
That You Shouldn't Miss
ISBN 978-3-7408-0598-2

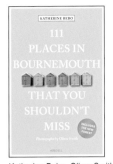

Katherine Bebo, Oliver Smith
111 Places in Bournemouth
That You Shouldn't Miss
ISBN 978-3-7408- 1166-2

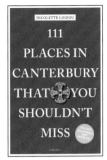

Nicolette Loizou
111 Places in Canterbury
That You Shouldn't Miss
ISBN 978-3-7408-0899-0

Philip R. Stone
111 Dark Places in England
That You Shouldn't Miss
ISBN 978-3-7408-0900-3

John Sykes, Birgit Weber
111 Places in London
That You Shouldn't Miss
ISBN 978-3-7408-1644-5

Solange Berchemin,
Martin Dunford, Karin Tearle
111 Places in Greenwich
That You Shouldn't Miss
ISBN 978-3-7408-1107-5

Nicola Perry, Daniel Reiter
33 Walks in London
That You Shouldn't Miss
ISBN 978-3-95451-886-9

Kirstin von Glasow
111 Gardens in London
That You Shouldn't Miss
ISBN 978-3-7408-0143-4

Laura Richards, Jamie Newson
111 London Pubs and Bars
That You Shouldn't Miss
ISBN 978-3-7408-0893-8

Emma Rose Barber,
Benedict Flett
**111 Churches in London
That You Shouldn't Miss**
ISBN 978-3-7408-0901-0

Solange Berchemin
**111 Places in the Lake District
That You Shouldn't Miss**
ISBN 978-3-7408-0378-0

Rob Ganley, Ian Williams
**111 Places in Coventry
That You Shouldn't Miss**
ISBN 978-3-7408-1044-3

Martin Booth, Barbara Evripidou
**111 Places in Bristol
That You Shouldn't Miss**
ISBN 978-3-7408-1612-4

Alexandra Loske
**111 Places in Brighton and
Lewes That You Shouldn't Miss**
ISBN 978-3-7408-1727-5

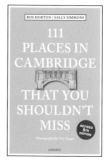

Rosalind Horton,
Sally Simmons, Guy Snape
**111 Places in Cambridge
That You Shouldn't Miss**
ISBN 978-3-7408-1285-0

Justin Postlethwaite
**111 Places in Bath
That You Shouldn't Miss**
ISBN 978-3-7408-0146-5

Gillian Tait
**111 Places in Edinburgh
That You Shouldn't Miss**
ISBN 978-3-7408-1476-2

Tom Shields, Gillian Tait
**111 Places in Glasgow
That You Shouldn't Miss**
ISBN 978-3-7408-1488-5

Gillian Tait
111 Places in Fife
That You Shouldn't Miss
ISBN 978-3-7408-1740-4

Kai Oidtmann
111 Places in Iceland
That You Shouldn't Miss
ISBN 978-3-7408-0030-7

Andrea Livnat,
Angelika Baumgartner
111 Places in Tel Aviv
That You Shouldn't Miss
ISBN 978-3-7408-0263-9

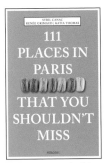

Sybil Canac, Renée Grimaud,
Katia Thomas
111 Places in Paris
That You Shouldn't Miss
ISBN 978-3-7408-0159-5

Thomas Fuchs
111 Places in Amsterdam
That You Shouldn't Miss
ISBN 978-3-7408-0023-9

Rüdiger Liedtke
111 Places in Mallorca
That You Shouldn't Miss
ISBN : 978-3-7408-1049-8

Alexia Amvrazi,
Diana Farr Louis, Diane Shugart,
Yannis Varouhakis
111 Places in Athens
That You Shouldn't Miss
ISBN 978-3-7408-0377-3

Christine Izeki, Björn Neumann
111 Places in Tokyo
That You Shouldn't Miss
ISBN 978-3-7408-1277-5

Christoph Hein, Sabine Hein
111 Places in Singapore
That You Shouldn't Miss
ISBN 978-3-7408-0382-7

Jo-Anne Elikann
111 Places in New York
That You Must Not Miss
ISBN 978-3-95451-052-8

Evan Levy, Rachel Mazor,
Joost Heijmenberg
111 Places for Kids in New York
That You Must Not Miss
ISBN 978-3-7408-1218-8

Andréa Seiger, John Dean
111 Places in Washington
That You Must Not Miss
ISBN 978-3-7408-1560-8

Kim Windyka, Heather Kapplow,
Alyssa Wood
111 Places in Boston
That You Must Not Miss
ISBN 978-3-7408-1558-5

Amy Bizzarri, Susie Inverso
111 Places in Chicago
That You Must Not Miss
ISBN 978-3-7408-1030-6

Amy Bizzarri, Susie Inverso
111 Places for Kids in Chicago
That You Must Not Miss
ISBN 978-3-7408-0599-9

Floriana Petersen, Steve Werney
111 Places in San Francisco
That You Must Not Miss
ISBN 978-3-7408-1698-8

Laurel Moglen, Julia Posey,
Lyudmila Zotova
111 Places in Los Angeles
That You Must Not Miss
ISBN 978-3-7408-0906-5

David Doroghy, Graeme Menzies
111 Places in Vancouver
That You Must Not Miss
ISBN 978-3-7408-0494-7

This book is a team effort. Alistair Layzell provided the early inspiration, Laura Olk at the Emons office made it happen, Ros Horton turned my word salad into English and Karin Tearle shot an astonishing array of photographs. Then there are the indispensable friends and relations: Patti-Pea, Katy Walsh Glinert, John Breslin, Michael Hutchison, Emma Marigliano, Juliet Rose, Simon Rose, David Stone and Lindsay Sutton.

Ed Glinert is Britain's most prolific tour guide, working in London, Manchester and Liverpool. He is a celebrated author (*Penguin's London Compendium*, 2003), cruise ships speaker and Arts Society lecturer. He is a highly-experienced journalist who worked for *Private Eye* magazine for more than 10 years. This is his third 111 book after London's East End and Yorkshire.

Karin Tearle has a BA in French and Italian from Goldsmiths, University of London, is a trustee of the Rwanda Development Trust, and has an affinity with Greenwich where she lives. Karin is social secretary of Aperture Woolwich Photographic Society, one of the oldest clubs in the country, and is extremely passionate about photography.